CW00350436

THE SLEEPING LORD AN

had all
within that reaching prism
one patria:
rooted clod or drifted star
dog or dryad or
man born of woman

did the sacred equation square the mundane site
was truth with fact conjoined
did the earth-mother
blossom the stone lintels
did *urvus* become *urbs*
did the bright share
turn the dun clod
to the star plan
did they parcel out
per scamna et strigas
the *civitas* of God
that we should sprawl
from Septimontium
a megalopolis that wills death?

Does the pontifex, do our lifted trumpets, speak to the city and
the world to call the tribes to Saturnalia to set misrule in the
curule chair, to bind the rejected fillet on the King of the Bean?
It's hard to trapes these things
from the circuit of the agger
from the traverse of the wall
waiting for the middle watch to pass
wanting the guard-house fug
where the companions nod
where the sooted billikin
brews the night broth

so cold it is, so numb the intelligence,
so chancy the intuition, so alert the apprehension for us who walk
in darkness, in the shadow of the *onager*, in the shadow of the

13

labyrinth of the wall, of the world, of the robber walls of the world city, trapesing the macrocosmic night.

Or, trapesing the night within, walking the inner labyrinth where also the night is, under the tortoise of the skull, for every man walking?

Under the legionary's iron knob, under the tribune's field crest, under the very distinguished gilt *cassis* of the Legatus himself?

We don't know the ins and outs

how can we? how shall we?

What did our mothers tell us? What did their mothers tell them? What the earth-mother told to them? But what did the queen of heaven tell *her*?

What was it happened by the fire-flame eating the griddle-cake . . . or by the white porch where out sister sang the Sabine dirge.

. . . they used to say we marched for Dea Roma behind the wolf sign to eat up the world, they used to say we marched for the Strider, the common father of the Roman people, the father of all in our walk of life, by whose very name you're called . . .

but now they say the Quirinal Mars turns out to be no god of war but of armed peace. Now they say we march for kind Irene, who crooks her rounded elbow for little Plutus, the gold-getter, and they say that sacred brat has a future . . .

now all can face the dying god
the dying Gaul
without regret.

But you and me, comrade, the Darlings of Ares, who've helped a lot of Gauls and gods to die, we shall continue to march and to bear in our bodies the marks of the Marcher – by whatever name they call him . . .

we shall continue to march
round and round the cornucopia:

that's the new fatigue.

c. 1952, but using, in part some fragments written c. 1940.

DAVID JONES

The Sleeping Lord

and other fragments

FABER & FABER

First published in 1974
by Faber & Faber Ltd
Bloomsbury House
74–77 Great Russell Street
London WC1B 3DA
This paperback edition first published in 2017

Printed in England by TJ International Ltd, Padstow, Cornwall

A CIP record for this book is available from the British Library

ISBN 978-0-571-33951-8

2 4 6 8 10 9 7 5 3

PUBLISHER'S NOTE

'A, a, a, Domine Deus' appeared in the David Jones issue of *Agenda*, Vol. 5, Nos. 1-3, Spring–Summer, 1967. Part of this poem was first printed in the essay, *Art and Sacrament, Epoch and Artist* (Faber, 1959).

'The Wall' was first published in *Poetry*, LXXXVII, No. 2 (November 1955).

'The Dream of Private Clitus' first appeared in *Art and Literature*, No. 1 (March 1964).

'The Fatigue' was privately printed by Will and Sebastian Carter at the Rampant Lions Press, Cambridge, 'as a token of affection and esteem from friends and admirers of David Jones on the occasion of his seventieth birthday, November 1st, 1965'.

'The Tribune's Visitation' was first printed in *The Listener*, 22nd May, 1958. It was published as a book by the Fulcrum Press in 1969.

'The Tutelar of the Place' first appeared in *Poetry*, XCVII, No. 4 (January 1961).

'The Hunt' was first printed in *Agenda*, Vol. 4, No. 1(April–May, 1965).

'The Sleeping Lord' was first published in the David Jones Special Issue of *Agenda*, Vol. 5, Nos. 1-3 (Spring–Summer, 1967). This issue also reprinted 'The Wall', 'The Dream of Private Clitus', 'The Tutelar of the Place' and 'The Hunt'.

CONTENTS

A, a, a, DOMINE DEUS

I said, Ah! what shall I write?
I enquired up and down.
                  (He's tricked me before
with his manifold lurking-places.)
I looked for His symbol at the door.
I have looked for a long while
                  at the textures and contours.
I have run a hand over the trivial intersections.
I have journeyed among the dead forms
causation projects from pillar to pylon.
I have tired the eyes of the mind
                  regarding the colours and lights.
I have felt for His Wounds
                  in nozzles and containers.
I have wondered for the automatic devices.
I have tested the inane patterns
                  without prejudice.
I have been on my guard
                  not to condemn the unfamiliar.
For it is easy to miss Him
                  at the turn of a civilisation.
    I have watched the wheels go round in case I might see the
living creatures like the appearance of lamps, in case I might see
the Living God projected from the Machine. I have said to the
perfected steel, be my sister and for the glassy towers I thought I
felt some beginnings of His creature, but *A, a, a, Domine Deus*,
my hands found the glazed work unrefined and the terrible
crystal a stage-paste . . . *Eia, Domine Deus.*

c. *1938 and 1966.*

THE WALL

We don't know the ins and outs
        how should we? how could we?
It's not for the likes of you and me to cogitate high policy or to
guess the inscrutable economy of the pontifex
        from the circuit of the agger
        from the traverse of the wall.
But you see a thing or two
        in our walk of life
        walking the compass of the vallum
walking for twenty years of nights
        round and round and back & fro
on the walls that contain the world.

You see a thing or two, you think a thing or two, in our walk of
life, walking for twenty years, by day, by night, doing the rounds
on the walls that maintain the world

        on the hard tread of the silex
        on the heavy tread of the mound
up in the traversed out-work, stepping it at the alert, down on the
via quintana stepping it double-quick by numbers to break y'r
tiro-heart . . .
        dug in wrong side the *limes*
or walled in back at depot?

                                      it's evens, more or less
as far as jumping to it goes.

        But what about the Omphalos
there's the place for the proud walkers
        where the terminal gate
        arcs for the sections in column
stepping their extra fancy step
        behind the swag and spolia
o' the universal world

                              . . . out from The Camp

in through the dexter arch of double-wayed Carmenta
by where Aventine flanks The Circus
                        (from Arx the birds deploy?)
to where the totem mother
                        imported
                        Ionian
                        of bronze
brights Capitoline for ever
                                        (from the Faunine slope
of creviced Palatine does the grey wraith erect her throat to
welcome the lupine gens?)

Erect, crested with the open fist that turns the evil spell, lifting the
flat palm that disciplines the world, the signa lift in disciplined
acknowledgement, the eagles stand erect for Ilia
                        O Roma
                        O Ilia
                        Io Triumphe, Io, Io . . .
                        the shopkeepers presume to make
the lupine cry their own.
                                        The magnates of the Boarium
leave their nice manipulations. You may call the day ferial, rub
shoulders with the plebs. All should turn out to see how those
appointed to die take the Roman medicine. They crane their
civvy necks half out their civvy suits to bait the maimed king in
his tinctured vesture, the dying *tegernos* of the wasted *landa* well
webbed in our marbled parlour, bitched and bewildered and far
from his dappled patria far side the misted Fretum
                        You can think a thing or two
on *that* parade:
                        Do the celestial forechoosings
                        and the hard journeyings
come to this?
                        Did the empyreal fires
hallow the chosen womb
                        to tabernacle founders of
                        emporia?
Were the august conjoinings

                        was the troia'd wandering
                        achieved
did the sallow ducts of Luperca
                        nourish the lily white boys
was Electra chose
                        from the seven stars in the sky
did Ilia bear fruit to the Strider
                was she found the handmaid of the Lar.

Did the augurs inaugurate, did the Clarissimi steady the trans⁄
verse rods, did they align the plummets carefully, did they check
the bearing attentively, was the templum dead true at the median
intersection
                        did the white unequal pair
labour the yoke, tread the holy circuit
                                did they, so early
in the marls of Cispadana
                        show forth, foretoken
the rudiments of our order
                                when the precursors
at the valley⁄sites made survey of the loam, plotted the trapezoids
on the sodden piles, digged the sacred pits, before the begin⁄
ning . . .
                        did they square the hill⁄sites
for the hut⁄circles, did the hill⁄groups look to each other, were
the hostile strong⁄points one by one, made co⁄ordinate
                        did Quirinal with Viminal
call to the Quadrata
                        did the fence of Tullius
embrace the mixed kindreds
did the magic wall
                        (that keeps the walls)
describe the orbit

did that wall contain a world
                        from the beginning
did they project the rectilineal plane upwards
to the floor of heaven

THE DREAM OF PRIVATE CLITUS

'*The Dream of Private Clitus*' *is a fragment of a work. The setting is in some sort of a guard-post on the wall of Roman Jerusalem at the time of the Passion.*

Clitus is a soldier of long service, from the district of Rome itself.

His companion Oenomaus is a young soldier, not long recruited from Greece, from that part once called Elis, where the Olympia was.

The fragment consists entirely of a monologue by Clitus, except for ten words of an interrogatory nature.

Clitus is describing to his new companion a dream he had once had years before as a young legionary serving in a campaign in Germany. His mate at that time being a Celt, soon killed in action, called Lugobelinos.

The main motif of the fragment derives from that superb marble relief carving of Tellus Mater which formed one of the two panels (the other was the goddess Roma) on the east front of the Ara Pacis Augustae facing the Flaminian Way leading north from Rome; it was built on the Campus Martius, consecrated in the year B.C. 14, but dedicated in B.C. 9 when Augustus returned from campaigns in Spain and Gaul and was thought of as symbolising the Augustan "pacification of the world" (rather like the Palace of Peace at Geneva in our time).

I purposely make a Roman, a Celt and a Greek serving in the same Roman unit to symbolise the heterogeneous nature of the Empire. I do not know whether in fact this could have occurred at that date, probably not. I chose the name Clitus because to me it felt Roman, actually it is a Greek name, I may also have got it muddled up in my mind with Cletus whose name one hears each time one goes to a Mass of the Roman Rite, though that name too is I believe Greek. But I do not feel inclined to alter it now. I chose Oenomaus because it was the name of a king of Elis, son of the god Ares, in Greek Mythology and it did in fact remain a name among Greeks. I chose Lugobelinos for the Celt because it is the original Celtic form of the Welsh name Llywelyn, just as Cunobelinos was the actual name of Shakespeare's "radiant Cymbeline", in Welsh now Cynfelyn.

Once, on the Limes Germanicus, I dreamed: after a rear-guard, one of many. Extricating ourselves we were from the gods of those parts, no unusual thing. And, in my dream, the phantoms were all big bodied and bigly proportioned that leaned over me where I lay in a bivvy, next Lugo. '59 Lugo on our manipular roster, so Lugo he was, though his full, outlandish, Celtic nomen was Lugobelinos, a mouthful, worse than yours, Oenomaus. I take it you was wafted in from Arcady – gotta nymph for a sister?

All right! from Hollow Elis then, better still, a real, live, sprinting Olympian.

I'm from the Urbs – though reared a countryman.

Now, Celt or no, my Lugo fancied his weight as an inmate of our Asylum and reckoned himself as Ilian and as Urban as the Twins. May the blessed Manes rest him – a stray got him.

Well, there we were bivouacked, after five days in this rear-guard, and ours was the sinister flank, with the gods of those woods pressing in on us in among the trees of those woods. And where we lay it was as if we lay in a kind of peristyle, builded of the tall trees, deep within the shadowy labyrinth of those woods. Long corridors of arches stretched all ways. Smooth, straight boles those trees had, and no low growth with the sward between each as it were like a pavement. And it was as if the rounded arches of our basilicas were suddenly to bestir themselves and the genius of each column to exert itself and reach across toward the numen of the column opposite. For all is thrusting and directional in the labyrinth of those parts and each swaying limb of each tree struggles for the mastery, high up.

And looking up at those gusty vaults of the faded green of a dying year, with chinks of a now darkening blue, flecked from Westward with the caelian purple – for 'twas near toward the evening bugle – the mingle of their contesting boughs seemed to make pointed arches.

Now that's a thing you don't see in stone, Oenomaus, a pointed arch. And I don't suppose you ever will.
But it's a fine thing is a pointed arch made of the striving branches of the living wood.

And homing eagles winged above those windy arches and this, some of them reckoned, an auspicious sign and Lugo said: See, the Roman bird. But I said: Lugo, don't talk wet. Don't talk like a civvy who's arranged another war. And fell asleep.

And as I slept, I dreamed, and in my dream – well, it's small marvel I dreamed of large bodies, considering the farish bulk and long reach of the Chauci and the Langobardi and such like tow-haired great bastards. As milk-necked they are and as golden locked as any meretrix that brights a shady colonnade between Viminal and Esquiline, back home.
These big, fair-hued square-heads had hung on our exposed flank for five days. And when I say five days I mean the *last* five days of that delaying action. Five days, five weeks, why, five months we'd been up in those parts, a good five months we'd been in those parts before we got into this particular jamb.

So there I lay, and there I dreamed and in my dream, as I dreamed of the large limbs it seemed in my dream as if I no longer lay with Lugo in our bivvy under the pointed arches but now in my dream, with him and all fast sleeping – for in a sleep-dream you can dream of man sleeping and of a man waking, there's no end to the recessions, nor to the superimpositions neither, in these dreams. Anyway, in my dream-making we *now* lay in Mars Field, being carried thither by virtue of the genius of the dream, that's where we lay – outside the Ara Pacis in Mars Field, on the east side, flush under the outer wall of the east vestibule, as you come in from the Flaminian Road. There we lay in my dream under the white pentelic frieze, him now sleeping and I waking and the moon full on the gradual limbs of the marble goddess and on the chiselled folds of her marble linea and on the buoyant zephyrs that attend her, shadowy on the patient animals, clear on the exertive twins. It's to the life! Ever *seen* the Ara Pacis mate? When

you come in, by the Flaminian Gate? It's a fine job of work, all
that relief-work between the pilasters, but specially that left hand
one of the Terra Mater, specially under the full moon of the Ides
of April when they sacrifice, on her behalf, under her moon, the
creatures of kine as are womb-burdened at that time, and such
was the precise time in my dream-calendar – for there's no end to
the precision and exactitude of these dream-data. So, in my
dream, it was the round moon of the Fordicidia, and none other,
as shone bright on the worked pentelic.

You get a good relief in the moon of that type of work, it's a bit
of a marvel how they contrive that sort of work and that's a job
you'd be a fine duffer at, Oenamaus, mason-work. But that was
as fine a work as I've seen in the moon and that's a thing I should
never have seen in the ordinary run of things, but in these dreams
the fates arrange no end of comings together. Heavy bodies sail
the air with the greatest of ease in these dreams, there's no end to
the unions these sleep-dreams can lend to things separate enough
in wake-a-day.

And so it was that I, Private Clitus, in the first year of my service,
sleeping bivouacked next my butty – raw troops we were from the
last draft – in our flank-guard post, detached from best part of
our unit, fed up and far from sweetest home, a hundred miliaria
beyond the walls of the world – a hundred and more we were
from our transports in the estuary: we were based up there on
Lugdunum at the river mouth, well round beyond the Gaulish
Strait, half way to Thule – poor bleedin' orphans of the Mother
of Cities up there the Teutoburg Wood, at the fall of the year,
was privileged to be shown by the genius of sleep, the gestatrix
of each of us, depicted in marble, under her own moon on her
own special day at the gate of the city in the lent of the year.

This lune-light of my dream-night seemed to shine on the marble
zephyrs depicted there, drifting a-swan-back and on dolphin in
signification of the twin waters of the world, both marine and up
stream, narrow and wide, all the water-weirs and the netted seas
that Jove's Augustus fenced, for our perpetual health, shined also

on the leaning ears of the marble wheat-stalks and on the heaped fruits, on the peaceful ox, on the ewe sheep, browsing, and on all the fertile signification of the sculpture-work and on her, centrally seated with her marble *palla* well back from the marbles of her brow to show her marbled tresses, and the twin fruit of her, to clamber her calm lap, like the proper mother of us all, from whose containing deeps we come, to whose embrace we turn . . .

Twice as large and twice as natural she seemed under this moon – have you ever noticed that Oenomaus? These moons always make things twice as large and so it was with my dream-moon, all was as large again. Why, that outer wall at the precincts has no more than eighteen foot drop from the cornice, I'll be bound, but in my moon it seemed a good thirty foot looking up from our bivvy and the sculptured forms proportionately big and the shadows very deep and the brighted contours rounded and firm.

It was a fine sight to see, and, what's more, and now we're com-ing to it, out from the still marble, larger yet in her gradual appearing under the moon, she herself leaned in my dream and lightly her marble boys seemed yet suspended in the marble air, her seeming movement, for I saw no motion, seemed not to dis-arrange the placid forms depicted there, and that's a poser for waking-thoughts, but there's no end to the possibilities of these dreams. So at least she did *appear* to lean, detached as it were from the reliefwork and more bodily perceived, yet still in her static element of stone nor yet disturbing the balance of the masonry. And so she herself gravely inclined herself and seemed to reach her sizable marble limbs toward me and my mate in our bivvy, him sleeping and I waking, and the large uncertain phantoms of my dream that leaned over me up there in the Teutoburg became concrete in the proportioned limbs of Tellus Our Mother, lean-ing living from the east wall below the cornice and all the world seemed at peace deep within the folds of her stola as she leaned over our bivvy and all but touched our bivvy-sheets with her strong marble fingers.

And now, in my dream-thinking and by virtue of the vision or by the chancy ebb and flood of those dream tides that Oceanus charts, it seemed that me and Lugo were caught up into that peace, whether in a marble body I cannot tell, if as Dioscuri of flesh and blood, I can't say – the genius of the dream knows – but such ones we seemed to be as merited her large embrace for keeping, so it seemed to my dream-thinking, the Middle Watch at the traverse of the wall. It seemed that surely now for ever me and my battle-mate would be for ever in the lap of Tellus, high on the wall, within the gate, ageless emeriti, as a perpetual signification of Roma and her sons. And then we should watch the tyros sweat by each day to exercise, up there at Mars Camp, and – what discloses the nasty twist in the nature of us – I laughed right out at that, a last dream laugh.

And now (in my dream-now that is), from his side our gestatorial marble, Lugo cried out a name: Modron! he cries, and then, – but very low-voiced though: Porth-Annwfyn. Some numinous, arcane agnomen, but which to my dream-cognition was lucid as moonshine and did plainly signify: Gate of Elysium.

Now I knew no word of Lugo's lingo, and it was, after all, *my* dream, not his. Well, Oenomaus, what do you make of that one? But I'll tell you further: when they got him I was next by him in the traverse – and that was no dream – and he cried loud the same cult-name, but not the last bit, for he was done before he could utter it.

So, as I figure it, his Modron and our Matrona are one, and his *porth* that shadowy portal beyond which Proserpine abides, from fall till crocus-time.

But now at my sleep change, at the third transforming of the vision, at the final showing of the genius of the dream, at the cycle's end – the Horn Gate all but ajar – the chiselled folds of her stola that had seemed so white in the moon, were now, in the twinkling of an eye, become the coarse-wove folds rucked at the lap of just such an apron as the women use as part of the gear of their trade in the parts where I was born. And now the browsing

marble sheep next the marble ox, was now, at the turn of my
dream, the identical ewe‑lamb they took and trussed up for the
March Lucina Feast, one wet, windy morning when I was so
high.

It was a great day always in our part of the country, was the Juno
feast, but on this particular keen morning of her feast, on the First
of the ten calends of the Romulean year, I was playing Greeks
and Trojans with my brother, behind our byre, well under the
pent, you know:

> Mars wind, cold rain
> bairns and old‑bones
> best within,

when they came to take her away, and I bellowed for that lamb
– I well remember that – and so I *seemed* to bellow now, like a
bull, at my dream‑ending. But my dream‑bellowing turned out
to be the bawling of old Brasso, calling out the names and num‑
bers for the Middle Watch. There's no end to the metamorphoses
of these dreams.

Brasso? Brasso Olenius of No. 1 Cohort? The Primus Pilus Prior?

Why, yes, of course, who else but Brasso? Who else should shake
a man from such a dream? Of course he was up there with us,
he's always been with us, he always will be with us, while there's
any us to make memento of. Whether y're a half‑section in a
foreward cubby‑hole or half a cohort back in legion‑reserve,
there's always a Brasso to shout the odds, a fact‑man to knock
sideways and fragmentate these dreamed unities and blessed
conjugations, why certainly old Brasso was up there – and, he
was up the ladder, too, – the higher the casualties, the higher the
climber. There he was, in the *Primi Ordines* over‑night, and his
main leg up was the packet we got in that show and that's why,
after that show, we called him Brasso Germanicus, and then we
called him Brasso for short and that's why he's called Brasso to
this day. There's a bit of domestic reg'mental history for you and

you should have known that much with your one year of service, come the Kalends of Maius, Oenomaus.

Why, I reckon Brasso can persuade himself he was a tyro under the Divine Julius. For these fact-men, Oenomaus, have their hallucinations, don't forget that, indeed their delusions would beat a garret poet – only there's calculation in the very dreams of a Brasso.

Some say he was born shouting the odds, in full parade kit, with a pacing-stick under his cherubic little arm, in the year that Marius reorganized the maniples and put the whole works on a proper, professional, cohort footing.

<pre>
                            There *are* those that say
his mother laboured with him
                            in Anno Urbis Conditae
the year that measures
                            all the years.
They say that she
                            was ventricled of bronze
                            had ubera of iron
and that at each vigilia's term
she gave him of her lupine nectar
and by numbers.
And that a tart-mouthed salpinx
                            brayed unblown of mortal lips
its fierce Etrurian taratantara
                            at those routine hours
precisely.
And that, they say, is why
                            in actual, concrete
                            and present reality
                            we do, in fact
(at those four routine hours precisely)
                            relieve the guard.
To the beautiful cacophany of
                            those lancer-whiskered bloody bucinators
</pre>

22

when they start up on their convoking brass.

If his lovely face is purple it's to match the Legate's plume – and that's not done on a issue tot – that's the pigmentation of centuries. He's on the permanent establishment, if ever a climber was. But, when the Second Pleiad fails her light and Flora becomes exfoliate and the Urbs falls, you'll know that Brasso must have fallen previous – first at the peripheries of us, then at the very node:
That'ld be a difficult thing to dream, Oenomaus:

Dea Roma, Flora Dea
                  meretrix or world-nutricula
without Brasso.
                  There are some things
that can't be managed
                  even in these dreams.

c. 1960, but based, in part, on a longer work begun c. 1940.

THE FATIGUE
c.A.V.C. DCCLXXXIV
TANTVS LABOR NON SIT CASSVS

'*The Fatigue*' is one of some interrelated fragments which include '*The Wall*' and '*The Tribune's Visitation*' among other already published pieces.

The interrelatedness consists of each of these fragments being concerned with the Roman troops garrisoned in Syria Palaestina at the time of the Passion.

But in the case of '*The Fatigue*' the intrication with what the Roman Liturgy calls Feria V in Cœna Domini and Feria VI in Parasceve of the Great Week is more direct and obvious.

It would appear that our A.D. 1 post-dates the Incarnation by a few years and, as when writing '*The Anathemata*', I have supposed the Passion to have occurred about the middle year of Pilate's ten years procuratorship of Judaea and Samaria, shortly before the fall of Sejanus from power in Rome.

I have (as in each of the other fragments) made the personnel of the Jerusalem garrison to be of mixed recruitment. Thus the N.C.O. is from the Urbs herself, while some of his men are Celts from Gaul or Britain.

This may be felt to do violence to the historic facts or probabilities on more grounds than one and may call for a word of explanation.

I do not know whether or not recent research has modified the views of such authorities as Schürer, views which indicated that, apart from the governor's Praetorian Guard, the most likely troops available were Palestinian levies, such as the Sebastian Cohort, gentiles recruited in Samaria, Jews being exempt from service under the Roman Procurators, but not, presumably, under the native rulers, such as Herod Antipas.

There were no Legionary troops stationed in Palestine at that date.

But if I may have falsified some of the historical accidents I have done so with deliberation in order to convey a far more important historical truth: the heterogeneous composition of the forces of a world-imperium.

This unific aspect of an imperium is an essential element in '*The Dream of Private Clitus*', the other side of which coin, or rather that 'robbery' which Augustine speaks of as an inevitable concomitant of 'empire' I made some attempt to evoke in '*The Tutelar of the Place*', a piece which also belongs to these interrelated fragments.

With regard to all this I had in mind that inscribed stone found in the

24

Hauran area away east of the Jordan Valley and cited by George Adam Smith as a moving example of how men of all sorts and from all lands, among them Gauls and Teutons, were drafted for service far from their own green valley-ways.

I quote from memory and cannot recall the date of the inscription but I think it was somewhat later than the date of the Passion: '. . . born (?) and a lover of his country, having come from Germania, died serving with the Agrippian ala, was taken back to his own.'

I had also in mind other inscribed stones, one such I was shown in 1934 not far from Jerusalem. I was told that it was in situ and marked the site of the cook-house of some section of 'Legio X Fretensis', the legion whose Aquilifer had distinguished himself in the breaking shoal north-east of the South Foreland in 55 B.C.

That incised stone they showed to me was set up more than half a century after the Passion, for the Tenth Fretensis was not I understand posted to Judaea until the days of Trajan. None the less the sight of it brought the ordinary serving soldiers of First Century Roman Judaea very close to one especially owing to its alleged domestic-regimental use. And at the same time it brought back vividly to my mind those ill-scrawled inscriptions of the Forward Zone, equally domestic and regimental, marking at the turn of a duck-board track, the flimsy shelter that served as the cook-house of B Coy, nth Batt. R.W.F., or the painted board, set askew and pock-marked by stray bullet holes, which read: nth Field Coy. R.E. To gum-boot store. No loitering by day. But what a fall in the calligraphy.

There is evidence from other incised stones of a cohors Italica serving in the province of Syria though these too are, I think, of slightly later date than the Passion. But they inevitably recall 'the Italian band' stationed at Caesarea Palaestinae (where the procurators resided) whose centurion, Cornelius, is a hinge-figure in the history of the ecclesia, and whom I have often thought of as the third in a kind of 'apostolic succession' of centuriones.

The first being he who said 'I am a man subject to authority' and whose Domine, non sum dignus reverberates, as yet, in our Mass, though it was not introduced into our Roman Rite until a thousand years after the last Roman centurion 'was taken back to his own'.

The second in that succession of three being the unnamed centurion whose Vere hic homo justus erat is recorded by the author of the Fourth Gospel as having been said at the consummation of the event, in which my *fatigue-party is involved, in a Mars month on a Venus day, the noon-dark of which a 16th century Welsh poet evoked with untranslatable conciseness:* wybren ddu bryn Iddewon, *literally: sky black, Jews' hill.*

We might perhaps recall also that our key term, sacramentum, *was used of the enlistment-oath of the legionaries and that terms such as* milites Christi *and* militia coelestis *are not without undertones evocative of a decidedly uncelestial soldiery of a ruthless, this-world domination. Apart from analogies in the writings of the great Jewish Apostle of the Gentiles, it would seem that the powerful Carthaginian patristic writer, whose cast of mind many of us find unattractive and who in later life broke away from the unity of the Church, gave impetus to such semantic associations. And this may not be wholly unconnected with the fact that he, Quintus Septimius Florens Tertullianus, was the jurist son of a* centurio proconsularis.

This fragment, 'The Fatigue', while not formally divided into parts does as it were, 'change gear' at two points and so could be said to fall into three sections.

For the first ninety lines or thereabouts a Roman principalis *(identified in my mind with a Cockney N.C.O.) is speaking, apart from some twenty interspersed lines spoken by one or other of two privates of Celtic recruitment.*

The next hundred or so lines (commencing at 'on the narrow beat of the wall') is a soliloquy or reflection made in the context of Catholic Xtian tradition and theology upon an event which, for the soldiers involved, was but one more guard, fatigue or escort duty. Part of this soliloquy includes also the imagined reflections of one of the personnel.

The next seventy or more lines (beginning at 'From where beyond the Composite façade') switch abruptly away from the location of the fatigue-party to the central administration of the world-power and the departmental offices in Rome, at that date in the grip of the minister Sejanus and his security-police, though his liquidation by Tiberius (then on Capri) was imminent. The final seventeen lines of this concluding section return to the location and allocation of the men detailed.

Harrow
August 18th 1965
The Feast of Flavia Julia Helena, Saint and Empress.

GWANWYN YN Y LLWYN

ARBOR AXED FROM ARBOUR-SIDE
   THAT NOW STRIPT
IS MORE ARRAYED
MORE THAN IN THE SILVAN RIDE
   WHEN TO PIERCE THE GREEN
AND TANGLED TENEBRAE
   COMES APOLLO'S RAY
SEE WHAT SHEEN THE LOPPED BOUGHS
NOW LIFT HIGH
   ...FRONDE, FLORE, GERMINE
O CRUX AVE
   AVE VEXILLUM

Relief details, halt!
Fall out first file for this post
                          re∕mainder, order arms.
Nothing to report?
Nothing, sergeant, all very quiet, sergeant
                          bar a movement, out beyond
by the Water Gate, a bit back.

   Water Gate? what's that to you? that's Virgin Post area.
You save y'r eyes for trouble where the're detailed.
Not seen the ghost
                     of Judas Máchabee
b' any chance?
   D'you reckon you're tutelar deity of the whole of Salem City,
Upper and Lower and extra∕mural perimeter as well? Not
Water Gate nor Fish Gate neither, but from somewhere left of
Old Gate to right of the Arx, Birket Post West inclusive, with
y'r centre on Skull Hill, that's your bit of frontage
                     Skull Hill's your lode
the tump without the wall.
   Project an imagined line from that tump, cutting Cheese
Gully[1] back to this same block of silex where you now stand
and you've got y'r median point of vision – now hold it.
                     That's how we keep
the walls of the world
                     sector by sub∕sector
maniple by maniple
                     man by man,
                     each man as mans the wall
is as each squared, dressed stone
                     fronting the wall but one way
according to the run of the wall.
   It's whoresons like you as can't keep those swivel eyes to front
one short *vigilia* through as are diriment to our unific and expand∕
ing order.

   [1] Cf. the Tyropoeon Valley, the declivity which ran north∕south through the
Upper and Lower divisions of the city and means the valley of the cheese∕makers.

A few like you can undo
                and properly bitch
all the world plan
                though Jove himself
direct our august ordering.
                And keep that weapon
at the regulation slope
                when you're being addressed
b' a *principalis*[1]
                on his way to promotion
                let's hope.
    And you can report for *optio's*[2] party immediate, on relief of
guard, that's *now*. He wants a few extra details at the Water
Gate and seeing you're so attracted to the Water Gate, why then.
for once in y'r twenty years service your duties may fit y'r desires,
We'll see.
And where's that other beauty?
                where's Castor for our Pollux?
    Where's that insubordinate Gallic buddy of yours from fer
beyond The Province – what's his name? Crixus or some such,
'73 Crixus
                where's Crixus?
I warrant you two've been at it
                in some *lingua*
of the fog-bound *insula*
                half the *vigilia* through
but I waste breath on you
                where's Crixus?

    At his post, sergeant, should be. Next the munition-hoist that
does serve the Medium Donkey.[3]

[1] There were below the rank of centurion innumerable grades denoted variously
by *principales* and *immunes*. In text I equate this *principalis* with what in our army
would be a platoon-sergeant.
   [2] The *optiones* were assistant centurions. Each centurion had one *optio* to assist
him or take over from him.
   [3] I am assuming that the missile-throwing engine called the *onager* might, as with
our mortars, be of three categories: light, medium and heavy.

                    Man at hoist stands fast at hoist
that is Standing Orders, sergeant
                              leastways this quarter
of this moon, in this city
                         pending the Passage
                         of their god.
   We're informed, ar'n't we!
are you a Gallatic initiate
                         of this Aramaean cult, or what?
                         Crixus!
    Coming, sergeant.
Nothing to report?
                         Nothing, sergeant, other than
a shadowy movement, of a sort.
From what direction?
                         and let's have it precise.
   Would be Virgin Post area
                         or thereabouts
sometime since.

So that's how it is.
                         Better than we'd supposed!
O admirable collaboration!
                         The celestial pair
see with one eye to-night
                         the synchronization's perfect
there's tally in the alibi.
                         The eagle eyes of
Caesar's horse-marines
                         see through stone and all
at movements that are no concern of theirs
                         you can make number two
for *optio*'s fatigue.
New guard, take over.
Party!
You two, fall in behind.
Party! in file to quarters, march.

                    Mind that step
the leading file
this is the Procurator of Judaea's night-relief
stepping the smooth-laid silex of the wall
                    not the radiant Cymbeline's
                    trousered Catuvellauni[1]

having a cut at
                    the *passus Romanus*

pick 'em up in front!
                    Keep that regulation step . . .

                         \\

on the narrow beat of the wall
                    this relief of all
and two of you detailed
                    and the least of you
for escort without the gate
                    where the *optio* waits
his full complement
    And others of you to be detailed
                    (not on other fatigues)
for the spectacle
                    at the sixth hour
in Supplementary Orders
                    not yet drafted
to furnish, for the *speculatores*[2]
                    those who handle the instruments
who *are* the instruments

[1] The Catuvellaunian King, Cunobelinos, who began his reign about A.D. 5
was steadily rising in power at the time of the Crucifixion. He extended his rule
over large parts of south-east Britain and under him contacts with the Roman world
developed and his coinage seems to have been based on that of Augustus. He was
still reigning when in A.D. 40 troops and transports were assembled at Boulogne
for an immediate assault which was countermanded at the last moment. He died
shortly before the actual Claudian invasion of A.D. 45. His successors were of
divided counsel, some Romanophiles, others, such as Caratacos, determined to
resist. It is the same old story: the imperial power knew just when to strike with the
certainty of success.

[2] Here *speculatores* refers to a special branch of the service directly responsible to
the provincial governor for the carrying out of executions.

                    to hang the gleaming Trophy
on the Dreaming Tree[1]
                    and to see
on the leaning *lignum*
                    the *spolia*-bloom
where shine the Five Phálerae[2]
                    that till the hard war
and for his racked-out limbs
                    (*Extensis manibus . . .*)[3]
the dark-bright *armillae*[4]
                    Quis est vir qui habet coronam?[5]
for the spined-dark wreath
                    squalentem barbam
without the circuit-wall
                    of his own *patria*.[6]
                    Where the Spoil of Spoils
hangs to Iuppiter
                    and the trophies
are the Conqueror
                    . . . himself to himself
on the Windy Tree.[7]

[1] Cf. the Anglo-Saxon poem known as 'The Dream of the Rood', which, even in translation, seems to me to far excel any subsequent English poem about the Passion. The only thing with which one can compare it is the *Vexilla regis* written a century and more earlier and in a very different *milieu*. And something in two Welsh hymns of recent times, *Bryn Calfaria* and *Tydi, a roddaist* capture in their quite different way a similar intensity of feeling.

[2] The term *phalerae* was used of those discs awarded as battle honours, seen on the standards and, in smaller form, on the bodies of individual soldiers.

[3] These words are part of the rubric *Extensis manibus prosequitur*, directing the celebrant to extend his hands while continuing the prayer beginning *Supra quae propitio*, which follows the Consecration and pleads that the sacrifice may be acceptable as 'that which thy high priest Melchisedech offered up to thee'.

[4] *armillae* here refers to those armlets awarded for distinguished acts of individual bravery.

[5] This is a translation of a line in a poem by the 14th Century Welsh poet Gruffudd Gryg, reading: *Pwy yw'r gwr piau 'r goron*, 'who is the man that owns the crown?'

[6] Cf. Vergil. *Æneid* II 277-279. 'His beard made squalid, his hair concreted with blood, bearing the many wounds he had received round the circuit-wall of his own *patria*.'

[7] See the Nordic *Havamal*: 'I know that I hung on the windy tree for nine

Perhaps they'll serve you the heavier pick, the pounding
tamper, the spoil-shovels, the heavy maul
                                        the securing tackle
of purchase, of lift, of haul
                                        of stay
                                        against a Fall.
  It is weighty impedimenta
                                        that belongs to Laverna's[1] crux-gear
                                        it's no light-fatigue
you're in for.
  But perhaps, if you hang back behind Lanky, or make yourself scarce at the hand-out, you may get away with the lighter
essentials:
                                        the Four Hooks
                                        of Danubian iron[2]
along with a few spares
                                        in a wattled basket
shipped from Thames
plaited under the pluvial skies
                                        of Lear's *insula*
interweaved under the laddery rays
                                        that grace all fluvial Thulé
                                        so light a *bascauda*[3]
                                        as any child
might carry up a hill
                                        with briary-gifts
for the hill-god
                                        who, from the iron briars
                                        plucks flowers for all
so clinking light they are

whole nights, wounded with the spear, dedicated to Odin, myself to myself.' A
translation to this effect is given by Frazer in *The Golden Bough*, in the volume called
Adonis, Attis, Osiris.
    [1] Laverna was the tutelary goddess of malefactors.
    [2] The Illyrian and Danubian provinces provided much of the iron used in the
Roman Empire.
    [3] Cf. Welsh *bascawd* from *bascauda*. Martial, in one of his Epigrams, in sending a
present to a friend speaks of it being in a *bascauda* made by Britons and now put
to a Roman use.

to staple such a burdened bough
on world-orchard wall.

Or, inessentials, lighter still:
the tall reed from up-stream reaches
the sea-sponge from tidal Syrtis[1]
the small crock

of permitted dope
that compassioning Rachels fetch
from Mercy Seats.[2]

Or, may be, they'll detail you
for *stauros*-guard as well (that will depend on
details available)

and it will come
your turn
to stand alone under the meridian eye
between the Man Hanged
and the Joker.
Between the many eyes

that seem as eyes
in rodent-masks

when scrutting feet
swarm up from world-*cloaca*
and the spilled beauty
on the flowering transom.
Under the burning sky

between the tribal scape-beast
a male of the first year
in his murex-dyed lemniscus
and the tribe.
Between the pinioned substitute

[1] Although the Mediterranean is popularly regarded as having no tidal fluctuation worth mentioning, I understand that round about Syrtis, from which waters the Romans got a lot of their sponges, there is a bit of tide, which, if I remember aright, was mentioned in connection with operations in that area in World War II.

[2] Some years back I read, I think in Schürer, that there was a guild or sorority of pious Jewesses who on compassionate grounds provided a potion to dull the senses of felons sentenced to crucifixion.

absque macula[1]
　　　　　and the world-tribe
all *gentes*, every sept and kin
　　　　　humani generis.
Beneath the implacable ray
　　　　　that beats
　　　　　where y'r scorching back-plates rivet
　　　　　that beats
where the swarming flies
　　　　　pattern black
　　　　　the thirsting Yggdrasill[2]
　　　　　In ara crucis torridum
he Frees the Waters.[3]

　　　　　You will sag at the slope
between the Anathema and the Common Will?
　　　　　you will not
　　　　　(the *optio* 'll see to that)

[1] Cf. the scapegoat sent into the wilderness carrying the sins of the Israelitish tribes and the passover lamb that had to be a male of the first year without blemish and the *lemniscus* of the Classical world, the strip of textile dyed purple and twined round the crown of the supreme victor in various contests.
　I had in mind also that similar woollen red-dyed band called the *infulla* which was tied round the head as an insignia of honour and especially of priests and priestesses of Romano-Hellenistic cults and of victims about to be sacrificed. It is still with us, for the two strips of textile that hang from the mitres of bishops and abbots are still called *infullae*.
[2] The ashtree of Northern Mythology which reached to the heavens, had its roots in the earth and in the under-world and from the boughs of which dripped the hydromel.
[3] The Latin is quoted from a line in an early hymn. I don't know whether, by now, its date has been precisely determined, but some years back it was placed well before the 8th Century and de la Taille thought that the suggestion made by a German writer in 1841 to the effect that it was a hymn sung in the early church by newly baptised catechumens was not far out, for it begins *Ad coenam agni providi* and refers to the white robes of those about to participate in this Supper of the Lamb. The *ara crucis* or Altar of the Cross was in various centuries conceived of being as it were a grid set in the flames of the Passion making possible the life-giving bread.
　The figure associated with the wasted lands and the freeing of the waters, known to romance literature as Percival, is in the Welsh deposits called Peredur 'of the steel weapons'. He, or someone of the same name, bears also the significant agnomen or epithet, Penfeddyg, 'chief physician'.

you will stand at the ready
                              and hold them
                              if need be
at a pilum's length
                              for sometimes the stouter
more resolute or more slippy
                              would trespass
                              the marked-out *adytum*
            (where the stripped *mensa*
                              is set up
                              where the long *lancea*
                              obliquely thrust
must drain the Cup
                              for here
                              is *immolatio oblata*.)[1]

Should they press you back
                              against the Thing
                              lifted up

[1] As this passage in brackets is a hinge-passage I ought perhaps to say that the term *immolatio oblata* is used to describe the actual bodily immolation on the unlit Altar of the Cross of what had already been oblated at the lighted and festal board in the Supper-Room, which oblative act committed the Offerand to his actual immolation on the morrow and by his command "Do this" committed his *ecclesia* to the offering at her lighted altars of what had been immolated once and for all on the dark Hill.

This note is beginning to read like a theological treatise, whereas all I wish to make plain is that in writing the text I did so as a layman entirely indebted to ideas and terms borrowed from a theologian who forty-four years ago (1921) provided what seemed to me to be an aesthetic wholeness, a comprehensible, almost tangible unity to various propositions of our religion touching the relationship between the Mass, Calvary and the Supper. As might perhaps be expected of a Gaul, he, Maurice de la Taille gave an unific wholeness of form to what before one had accep-ted, but (how shall I put it?) had not apprehended in what exact sense the sequence of acts while being other were yet one and one yet other.

Moreover his exposition did, for me, in the early 1920s open windows and made sense of relationships altogether outside the immediate context of his strictly theo-logical thesis.

My impression is that more recent writers barely, if at all, mention him. I am no theologian and can only suppose they have their reasons for this silence. My concern here is only to indicate the source of my borrowed ideas and to render my tribute.

I feel I ought also to mention an old friend, Fr. Martin C. D'Arcy S.J., who

within the space measured
                    per pedes et passus
from the centred stake
                    but⁄end or war⁄head
don't signify, use either
the orders is: 'See you keep clear the defined orbis'
of the place
                    of anathémata.
  There, within the demarking *termini*[1]
                    in that place
which little Ginger the Mountain
                    the Pretanic fatigue⁄wallah
          (shipped in a slaver to Corbilo⁄on⁄Liger[2]
                    marketed at Massilia)
calls in his lingo

in 1926, in *The Mass and the Redemption*, used de la Taille's thesis as the groundwork
for what he had to say, which book justified what I had felt on first hearing the
bare outline of that thesis some years previously when it was under very bitter assault
from some quarters.
  [1] *per pedes et passus* was the formula used in measuring any space and *termini* or
cippi was used of the stones demarking any boundary. In text it is used of the stones
demarking the area or *orbis* within which the execution was carried out.
  A dozen lines earlier I refer to this area as 'the marked⁄out *adytum*' − the inner
sanctuary from which issued oracles, but this of course has reference to what that
particular place of execution was and is as seen in the context of Christian dogma.
That is why *adytum* is immediately followed by 'where the stripped *mensa* is set up,
etc'.
  [2] Corbilo at the mouth of the Loire, now St Nazaire, was I believe one of the
ports at which cargoes of tin shipped from Cornwall were unloaded for transport
overland, but that traffic appears to be associated with the pre⁄Roman period. The
Romans seem not to have worked the Cornish tin mines until the 3rd Century
A.D., not, at least, extensively.
  However, the geographer, Strabo, who would be about sixty when our Lord
was born, refers to Carbilo as being one of the more important of the ports of what
was then Roman Gaul.
  So 'little Ginger the Mountain' might easily, in the reign of 'the radiant Cym⁄
beline' have been sold along with boar⁄hounds and horses, shipped to Gaul sold
at Marseilles to find himself the property of a Roman of some sort serving in Judaea.
  Or, by then, he might have been a freedman serving with the forces of an
imperium which would not for some three or four decades yet hold within its recti⁄
lineal grid the valley⁄ways of green Siluria or displace with mass⁄produced coarse,
boring, megalopolitan wares the vital, asymetric, abstract beauties of the Bronze or
late Iron Age forms of his native *tref* in the hills of Orddwy − known to later
history as Meirionnydd or Merioneth.

                    Lle'r Benglog.[1]
    There, in that place
                    that will be called
                    The Tumulus[2]
you will complete the routine.

From where behind the Composite façade, off the second
quadrangle, past the third invisible cordon, covered by the
screened vent in the new oblique wall, far side the temporary
barrier, close the convenient niche where the sentinel has dumped
his shiny, dark, tight-rolled *paenula* and the emergency buckets
dress by the right
                    without entablature
                    flush with the drab cement
the inconspicious door[3]
                    beyond the spiked gate
                    past the tenth check-point
gives inward on a stair
                    that's narrow
but of polished Lunic
                    the hand-rail is functional
but of serrated ivory and baluster'd ornate.

    From where beyond the ante-chambers, across the greater
atrium and the lesser, through the double hangings

[1] The words in Matthew's account of the Passion reading in A. V. 'that is to
say, the place of a skull' and in the Vulgate *'quod est Calvariae locus'* read in Welsh
'yr hwn a elwir Lle'r benglog' (sometimes printed *Lle y benglog*), the *e* in *Lle* (place)
is pronounced approximately like the English 'a' in 'laid'.
[2] The Church of the Holy Sepulchre is meant, for there one roof covers the
actual mound of execution and the actual burial chamber.
[3] This is not a misprint for 'inconspicuous'. The Roman Survey used the term
conspicio of a properly inaugurated site, and just as auspicious is formed on *auspicio*
+ us I saw no valid reason for not forming 'inconspicious' on in + *conspicio* + us.
It served exactly to evoke this well-screened, and indeed inconspicuous entry to the
guarded apartments of an able but sinister and inauspicious figure.
    In writing this part of 'The Fatigue' the similarity between 'then' and 'now' was
not far from my mind.

                              (check‑point Minotaur
the whispered counter‑sign for the day
                              is 'Capri')
within the most interior room, on the wide‑bevelled marbled
table the advices pile and the out‑going documents wait his
initials.

From where in the adapted wing the ply‑partitions cubicle the
marble spaces and utile fittings plug the gilt volutes and the night
rota is tacked to the fluted pilaster.

From where, in the corridored annexe the newly assembled
parts and the convenient furnitures already need replacement,
they sit the regulated hours in the conditioned air and enclose
with each directing chit a root of Saturn's Loathing,[1] special
spined, for every jack man in Urbs, throughout *orbis*.
   From where an high administration deals in world‑routine,
down through the departmental meander
                 winding the necessities and accidents
                              the ball rolls slowly
                              but it rolls
and on it your name and number.
   By how an inner cabinet plot the *mappa mundi* when key
officials and security agents forward their overlapping but dis‑
crepant graphs
   by whether the session
                              is called for after
                              or before, noon
   by whether a hypocaust has fouled its flues
   by how long the amphora is off the ice
   by whether the wind
                              blows moderate from trans‑Tiber

[1] Saturn's Loathing is or was in some parts of Britain a country name for the
corn‑buttercup or *Ranunculus Arvensis*, which is described by botanists as a corn‑
field weed with spiny outgrowths. Everything that harms the grain is hateful to
Saturn. And in a series of roundels painted by Burne‑Jones illustrative of flower‑
names he showed two armed men (I think horsemen) encountered in a cornfield to
illustrate Saturn's Loathing.

or with a nasty edge

               straight up the Tiburtina
to blight his special buds on Esquiline
and really find his kidneys
  by whether there's an 'r' in the month
  by how a shuffled pack divides
  by how *whose* intuition? works

              by the fixed constella'd courses
in conjunction with the bright Wanderers
  by which side he gets out of bed.

By routine decrees gone out from a central curia, re Imperial
Provinces East Command
  by how a Legate's executive
              complies in detail
  by the disposition of groups
             and units of groups
  by whether the Tribunus Militum
             'Z' Corps, 'X' Zone
             has or has not
his applied-for replacement-drafts
  by personnel available to an Orderly Officer

             by the personnel available
to the Orderly Officer for the week ending
             this Saturn's day
             the day
after to-morrow
       (and look! the red-dyed sky-drape
from over Bosra way[1]

---

[1] Factually considered the first intimations of dawn or a soldier on the walls of
Jerusalem would come from the sky a good deal south of the direction of Bosra, for
though Bosra is away east of Jerusalem it is as much north as east.

But I was of course thinking mainly of Isaias LXIII: Who is this that cometh up
from Edom with dyed garments from Bosra – *iste formosus in stola sua . . .* ? and:
Why is thy apparel red and thy vesture like theirs that tread the wine-press?

But I had also in mind the legionary fortress at Bosra (Bostra), not in existence
at the date of this fatigue, but under Trajan to become the great frontier station

                    to-morrow is already
putting on to-day.)
          By your place on a sergeant's roster
          by where you stand in y'r section
          by *when* you fall in
          by if they check you from left or right
          by a chance numbering-off
                    by a corporal's whim
          you will furnish
                    that Fatigue.

garrisoned by the 3rd Legion known as the Cyrenaica, the H.Q. of troops operating on the eastern limits of the empire, just as, some 2,600 miles to the north-west,
the 20th Valeria Victrix at Chester garrisoned the forts of the western limits in the
hills of Wales.

THE
TRIBVNE'S
VISITATION

DIXIT. AT

TARANTARA

TVBATERRIBILI

DAVID JONES

IDEM

IN ME

CIRCA

A.V.C. DCCLXXXIV

TALINOS
VNITA

AB INCARNE XPI MCMLXVII

FVLCRVM EDTN

NOTES ON THE INSCRIPTION

The centre words 'Idem in me', 'The same (holds good) for me' was the formula used in ratification of the 'sacramentum' or oath of allegiance taken on enlistment. Away back before B.C. 100 each man said these words individually in signification of a contract with an individual com-mander. But with the changed conditions of a regular standing army drafts of men were conscripted for some twenty years service and the 'sacramentum' was taken corporately by groups of newly drafted recruits.

This oath bound them to the service of the state, as such, so that with the establishment of the principate it bound them to the reigning Caesar who embodied every aspect of the state in his own person. Pontifex Maximus no less than Imperator – Divus Caesar. Hence to break the sacramentum was not only an offence against what we call 'good order and military discipline' but at a transcendental level it laid the culprit open to the avenging furies of the tutelary deities who presided over the fortunes of the Roman world-order.

The words round the margin 'At tuba terribili sonitu taratantara dixit', from Ennius, 'Annals', Bk II, 143, have been variously translated by Classical scholars, e.g. 'Hark! the trumpet with its alarming note has cried "taratantara".' and 'Hark! the trumpet with alarming tones said tarántaráb.' Another translator gives: 'And the trumpet in terrible tones taratantara blared.'

It will be seen that this single Latin line has an impact not easily rendered in translation. My reason for using it on the title page is that (along with 'Idem in me') it chances to evoke a number of things that fit the theme of 'The Tribune's Visitation'. It certainly stirs in me memories of Pte. 'Shenkins' 6th Platoon, 'B' Coy nth Battalion R.W.F.

'There she goes again, taratántará–ráb-ráb. It's always 'B' Company!' That particular grouse must be as old as armies.

But there is another matter. It is assuredly true that by convoking bugles the personnel of all armies are summoned to routine and other duties, without which no imperium could be built up. But it is also true that in the 'mythos' which we have received it is by the clamour of trumpets that walled places representative of whole cultures have been brought down. Nor is this notion confined to deposits from Classical sources. For example, early in the 12th century B.C. in the Cananaean lands far side

43

Mare Nostrum, the walls of one of the most ancient of inhabited sites fell to the blast of trumpets, as the Negro Spiritual recalls for us

> 'Joshua fit the battle of Jericho
> And the walls came tumblin' down'

just as, half a millennium later, the walls of Alba Longa in Latium fell to the 'clangor' of the trumpets of Tullus Hostilius in the Eightieth Year from the Foundation of the City.

THE TRIBUNE'S VISITATION

It may be as well to say that 'The Tribune's Visitation' is linked with certain other pieces such as 'The Wall' or 'The Fatigue' in that it is concerned with troops of the Roman garrison in Palestine in the earlier decades of the First Century A.D. But while in 'The Fatigue' the date is specific and the men concerned are accidentally involved in the Passion (the date of which is taken as the spring of A.D. 30) in this present piece of the surprise visitation of a Military Tribune to troops of his command it is envisaged as being in any year of those first few decades of the 1st Century. In 'The Fatigue' I take liberties with history in making the troops appear as legionaries and of mixed recruitment in order to evoke the heterogeneous character of the forces of a world imperium.

So in 'The Tribune's Visitation' I make the personnel praetorian troops of the Italica cohort (cf. 'the Italian band' stationed at Caesarea Palaestinae c. A.D. 40 mentioned in Acts X.i.) but I again make them of mixed recruitment and again this is for reasons inherent in this present fragment. The 'companion piece' of 'The Tribune's Visitation' might be said to be 'The Tutelar of the Place'.

Sir!
No sir, yes sir, Middle Watch Relief, sir.
Just come off, sir.
Yes sir.
Well, no sir, half an hour back, sir.
No sir, some from last levy
                                    some, redrafted.
No sir, from all parts, sir.
In particular?
I see, and you, sergeant?
The Urbs, sir, Regio 4, sir.
Fifteen years, sir, come next October Games.

October Games!
                        and whose games, pray, are these?
Some Judy-show

to make the flowers grow?

the April mocked man

crowned and cloaked

I suppose

going rustic are they[1]
under y'r very nose

and you good Cockney bred
born well in sound of the geese-cry
and with the Corona up, I see

and of the First Grade.

Where won? or was it an issue, sergeant?
On the German *limes*, sir.
And y'r bar?
On the German *limes*, sir, North Sector.
And the two torques?
On the same *limes*, sir, South Sub-Sector, sir, in front of Fosse
60, sir, the other . . .

Enough! I'm not asking for back-filed awards or press *communiqués*
– no doubt the *Acta*[2] gave you half a column on how plebian
blood's no bar to bravery – I know it all and backwards. But we'll
speak presently, you and I.

For now, where's this mixed bunch

of yours?

I have a word to say.

Yes sir, very good sir, Guard! Guard!
for inspection . . .
Cease man, cease!

[1] No direct reference is intended here to the mocking of our Lord, but to the
widespread annual practices of a saturnalian character at the Hilaria, a festival
connected with the goddess Cybele which fell at the Vernal Equinox. The practices could very considerably vary: from primitive cult rites involving the death of a
victim to mere horseplay. I suppose the practical jokes of only a little back on our
April Fool's Day were a last faint echo of similar equinoctial revels, themselves the
echoes of more formidable rites.

[2] This stands for *acta diurna*, a daily news bulletin circulated, or publicly displayed,
in Rome.

                    A liturgy too late
is best not sung.

                    Stand them at ease
                    stand them easy
let each of you stand each as you are
let these sleep on and take their rest
                    if any man can sleep
to equinoctial runes
                    and full-moon incantations.

You, corporal, stand yourself easy.
You, whose face I seem to know
                    a good Samnite face.
Private what? Pontius what?
A rare name too, for trouble.

And you with the Etruscan look
not Pte Maecenas by any chance?
No sir, 330099 Elbius, sir.

But with a taste for the boards, eh? We must remember that at
the reg'mental binge. That lorica back to front and y'r bared
flanks become you well – extremely funny and very like your
noble ancestors, unless the terracotta lies.

But all of you stand
                    I have a word to say.
First, a routine word
                    a gloss on the book
and no more, a sergeant's word – sergeant.

Men, when you are dismissed to quarters, it is to quarter-duties,
not to Saturnalia. The regulation rest's allowed, now get on to
those kits, on to those brasses. D'you think that steel's brought
from Toletum at some expense for you to let to rust – and those
back-rivets and under those frogs . . .

but must I do a corporal's nagging, must I be scold, like a second cook to pallid sluts beneath her, must I read out a rooky's list of do's and don'ts and speak of overlaps and where to buy metal/polish. Are there no lance/jacks to demonstrate standing orders?

            Does the legate need to do
what he delegates?

            Must those with curial charge
be ever prying on a swarm of vicars

            or nothing goes forward?
Must tribunes bring gunfire[1] to centurions or else there's no parade?

But enough: analogies are wearisome and I could analogise to the end of time, my Transpadane gradma's friend taught me the tricks. I'd beat the rhetoric of Carnutic conjurors and out/poet ovates from druid bangors farside the Gaulish Strait. But I'll be 'forthright Roman' as the saying goes, but seldom goes beyond the saying. Let's fit our usage to the tag – for once.

The loricas of Caesar's men

            should shine like Caesar
            back and front
whose thorax shines all ways

            and to all quarters
            to the world/ends
whether he face unstable Britain

            or the weighty Persians.
So that all of them say:

            Rome's back is never turned.

But a word more: this chitty's fire is built for section's rations,

[1] This term that survived from the Regular Army and was familiar enough to soldiers of the new armies throughout the 1914–18 War, may by now be obsolete.

not for warming backsides. Is Jerusalem on Caucasus? Are your Roman loins so starved that Caledonian trews were best indented for? Should all the aunts on Palatine knit you Canusian comforts, or shall we skin the bear of Lebanon and mount the guard in muffs?

Come! leave that chatter and that witch-wife song, that charcoal can well tend itself; now do you attend your several duties.

Guard, guard – at ease! Guard! . . .
No, sergeant, no, not so anxious
                      I have a word to say
I have a more necessary word.
I would bring you to attention
                      not liturgically
                      but in actuality.

The legate has spoken of a misplaced objectivity. I trust a serving officer may know both how to be objective and to judge the time and place. For me the time is now and here the place.

You sergeant, you junior N.C.O.s
                      my order was stand easy
men less at ease I've seldom seen.

It belongs to the virtue of rank to command. If I, by virtue of my rank, deem it necessary to command composure, then compose yourselves. I have a word to say for which a measure of composure may, in you, be requisite.

                      I have a word to say to you as men and

It was used of a brew of tea supposed to be available from the cook-house for men in barracks or camps in time for 'rouse-parade'.

49

as a man speaking to men, but, and a necessary but, as a special
sort of man speaking to a special sort of men at a specific but
recurring moment in *urbs*-time.

Is this a hut on Apennine, where valley-gossips munch the chest-
nuts and croak Saturnian spells? Is this how guard-details stand
by for duties who guard the world-utilities?

Old rhyme, no doubt, makes beautiful
                          the older fantasies
but leave the stuff
                          to the men in skirts
who beat the bounds
                          of small localities
all that's done with
                          for the likes of us
in *Urbs*, throughout *orbis*.

It's not the brotherhood of the fields or the Lares of a remembered
hearth, or the consecrated wands bending in the fertile light to
transubstantiate for child-man the material vents and flows of
nature into the breasts and milk of the goddess.

                          Suchlike bumpkin sacraments
are for the young-time
                          for the dream-watches
now we serve contemporary fact.

                          It's the world-bounds
we're detailed to beat
                          to discipline the world-floor
to a common level
                          till everything presuming difference
and all the sweet remembered demarcations
                          wither

to the touch of us
                              and know the fact of empire.
Song? antique song
                              from known⁄site
spells remembered from the breast?
                              No!

But Latin song, you'll say, good song the fathers sang, the
aboriginal and variant alliterations known to each small *pagus*.
The remembered things of origin and streamhead, the things of
the beginnings, of our own small beginnings.

                              The loved parts of that whole
which, when whole
                              subdued to wholeness
all the world.

These several streams, these local growths, all that belongs to the
fields of Latium, to the Italic fatherland, surely these things, these
dear pieties, should be remembered?

It stands to reason you'll say, these things, deep things, integral to
ourselves, make for efficiency, steady the reg'mental will, make
the better men, the better soldiers, so the better friends of
Caesar.

                              No, not so
that pretty notion, too, must go.
                              Only the neurotic
look to their beginnings.

We are men of now and must strip as the facts of now would have

it. Step from the caul of fantasy even if it be the fantasy of sweet
Italy.
Spurn the things of Saturn's Tellus?
Yes, if memory of them
                            (some pruned and bearing tree
                            our sister's song)
calls up some embodiment
                            of early loyalty
raises some signum
                            which, by a subconscious trick
softens the edge of our world intention.

Now listen: Soldiers, comrades and brothers, men of the Cohors
Italica, men of my command, guard-details, I address you.

I've never been one for the vine-stick, I've never been a sergeant-
major 'Hand-us-Another'[1] to any man. We can do without a
Lucilius in this mob, but we want no Vibulenuses neither.

I would speak as Caesar's friend to Caesar's friends. I would say
my heart, for I am in a like condemnation.

I too could weep
                            for these Saturnian spells
and for the remembered things.
                            If you are Latins
so am I.

If the glowing charcoals draw your hearts to braziers far from this
parched Judaean wall, does it not so draw my heart?

[1] I was thinking of the centurion mentioned in Tacitus' *Annals*, notorious for
breaking his vine-stick on the backs of his men and nicknamed by them *Cedo
alteram*.

If the sour issue tot
hardly enough to wet the whistle
yet calls up in each of you
                          some remembered fuller cup
                          from Luna vats
do not I too remember cups so filled
                          among companions?
                          the brews of known-site
                          and the vintage hymn
within a white enclosure
                          our side Our Sea?
No dying Gaul
                          figures in the rucked circus sand
his far green valley
                          more clear than do I figure
from this guard-house door
                          a little porch below Albanus.
No grave Teuton of the Agrippian *ala* rides to death on stifling
marl-banks, where malarial Jordan falls to the Dead Meer,
thinking of broad salubrious Rhine, more tenderly than do I
think of mudded Tiber.

And we've lesser streams than Tiber
                          and more loved
more loved because more known
                          more known
because our mothers' wombs
                          were opened on their margins
and our sisters' shifts
                          laved in the upper pools
and pommelled snowy
                          on the launder-banks.

These tributary streams we love so well make confluence with
Tiber and Tiber flows to Ostia and is lost in the indifferent
sea.

But Our Sea, you'll say, still *our* sea – you raise the impatient shout, still the Roman Sea, that bears up all the virtues of the Middle World, is tideless and constant, bringing the norm, without variation, to the several shores.

Are you party members
doped with your own propaganda?

Or poets who must need weave dreams and yet more dreams, saleable dreams, to keep the duns from doorstep, or have hearts as doting as those elder ministers who think the race of gods wear togas?

But you are soldiers
with no need for illusion
for, willy-nilly
you must play the appointed part . . .
Listen! be silent!
you *shall* understand
the horror of this thing.
Dear brothers, sweet men, Italian loves
it may not be.

We speak of ends and not of origins when Tiber flows by Ostia. The place is ill-named, for mouths receive to nourish bodies, but here the maw of the world sucks down all the variant sweets of Mother Italy and drains to world-sea the blessed differences: No longer the Veneti, no more Campanian, not the Samnite summer pipes nor the Apulian winter song, not the Use of Lanuvium nor the *Etrusca disciplina*, not Vetulonia of the iron fasces, not the Ayra of Praeneste in the gold fibulas, nor any of the things of known-site . . .

our world-Maristuran
marshals all to his world-sea.

Bucinator Taranus, swilling his quarter's pay with his Com-
brogean listing-mates, tough Lugobelinus and the radiant
Maponus[1] (an outlandish triad to wear the Roman lorica),
maudlin in their barrack cups habitually remember some high
hill-cymanfa; thus our canteens echo with:

> *'No more in dear Orddwy*
> *We drink the dear meddlyn'*[2]

or some such dolorous anamnesis.

Now we, for whom their Ordovician hills are yet outside the
world (but shortly to be levelled to the world-plain) must think
no more of our dear sites or brews of this dear *pagus*, or that known
enclosure loved of Pales, lest, thinking of our own, our bowels
turn when we are commanded to storm the palisades of others and
the world-plan be undone by plebeian pity.

As wine of the country

[1] The Celtic cult-figure Maponos was equated by Classical writers with Apollo.
Lugobelinos is said to be the Celtic form from which Llywelyn derives. The trum-
peter 'Taranus' needs some apology. I wrote it by a confusion with Tanarus which
occurs on one dedication-stone set up in Roman Chester where it is used as an
epithet of Jove, the supreme tutelar of the Roman imperium, the sky-god, Iuppiter
Optimus Maximus, whose cult was the official worship of the Roman state and
signified the Roman domination on earth. Other figures of the Roman pantheon
frequently shared altars with some local tutelar, but in this instance great Jupiter
himself is given a barbarian epithet, Tanarus, said to signify the god who roars, and,
if so, a Germanic form not dissimilar in meaning from the Roman Tonans, the
Thunderer. When writing *The Tribune's Visitation* I had in mind this inscription,
but thought it read not Tanaro but Tarano. This was owing to an association with
taran the Welsh word for thunder, But as, presumably, *taran* derives from some
much earlier Celtic form I decided to leave 'Taranus' uncorrected.

[2] cf. the traditional air *Of Noble Race was Shenkin* with the 18th(?) Century lines

> 'No more in dear Montgomery
> We drink the dear metheglin'

cymanfa – an assembly; pronouce cum-mán-vah.
The *dd* in Orddwy (the land of the Ordovices of central Wales) and the *dd* in
meddlyn is pronounced as English 'th' in 'then' or 'thou'. The form 'metheglin' is
an accepted anglicization.

                              sweet if drawn from wood
near to the living wood
                              that bore the grape
                              sours if taken far
so can all virtue curdle in transit
so vice may be virtue uprooted
so is the honey-root of known-site
                              bitter fruit for world-floor.

The cultural obsequies must be already sung before empire can masquerade a kind of life.

What! does Caesar mime?
                              are the world-boards his stage?
Do we, his actors, but mimic for a podium full of jeering gods what once was real?

That seems about the shape of it, O great Autocrator, whose commission I hold, but hold it I do, over and above the *sacramentum* that binds us all.

What then?
                              Are we the ministers of death?
                              of life-in-death?
do we but supervise the world-death
                              being dead ourselves
long since?

Do we but organize the extension of death whose organisms withered with the old economies behind the living fences of the small localities?

Men of my command, guard details of the Antonia, soldiers of our

Greater Europa, saviours of our world-hegemony, tiros or veterans, whichever you be, I have called you brothers, and so you are, I am your elder brother and would speak and command fraternally.

Already I have said enough to strip me of my office, but comrades, I did so from a full heart, from a bursting heart and knowing your hearts . . .

                but set the doors to
let's stand within
                and altogether
let's shut out
                the prying dawn

I have things to say
                not for the world-wind to bear away
but for your ears, alone, to hear.
                I have spoken from a burning heart
I speak now more cool
                (if even less advised)
within these guard-house ·walls
                which do, here and for us
enclose our home
                and we one family of one *gens*
and I the *pater familias*
                these standards, the *penates*
however shorn to satisfy
                the desert taboos
                of jealous baals.

This chitty's fire, our paternal hearth, these fatigue-men our sisters, busy with the pots, so then, within this sacred college we can speak *sub rosa* and the rose that seals our confidence is that red scar that shines on the limbs of each of us who have the contact with the fire of Caesar's enemies, and if on some of us that sear burns, then on all, on you tiros no less than on these *veterani*

for all are members
of the Strider's body.
                              And if not of one hope
then of one necessity.
For we all are attested to one calling
not any more several, but one.
And one to what purpose?
                              and by what necessity?

See! I break this barrack bread, I drink with you, this issue cup,
I salute, with you, these mutilated signa, I with you have cried
with all of us the ratifying formula: *Idem in me.*

                              So, if the same oath serve
why, let the same illusions fall away.

Let the gnosis of necessity infuse our hearts, for we have
purged out the leaven of illusion.
If then we are dead to nature
                              yet we live
                              to Caesar
                              from Caesar's womb we issue
by a second birth.

Ah! Lucina!
                              what irradiance
can you bring
                              to this parturition?
What light brights this deliverance?
From darkness
                              to a greater dark
the issue is.

Sergeant, that shall serve, for now.

THE TUTELAR OF THE PLACE

She that loves place, time, demarcation, hearth, kin, enclosure, site, differentiated cult, though she is but one mother of us all: one earth brings us all forth, one womb receives us all, yet to each she is other, named of some name other . . .

                                        . . . other sons, beyond hill, over strath, or never so neighbouring by nigh field or near crannog up stream. What co-tidal line can plot if nigrin or flax-head marching their wattles be cognate or german of common totem?

Tellus of the myriad names answers to but one name: From this tump she answers Jac o' the Tump only if he call Great-Jill-of-the-tump-that-bare-me, not if he cry by some new fangle moder of far gentes over the flud, fer-goddes name from anaphora of far folk wont woo her; she's a rare one for locality. Or, gently she bends her head from far-height when tongue-strings chime the name she whispered on known-site, as between sister and brother at the time of beginnings . . . when the wrapped bands are cast and the worst mewling is over, after the weaning and before the august initiations, in the years of becoming.

When she and he 'twixt door-stone and fire-stane prefigure and puppet on narrow floor-stone the world-masque on wide world-floor.

When she attentively changes her doll-shift, lets pretend with solemnity as rocking the womb-gift.

When he chivvies house-pet with his toy *hasta*, makes believe the cat o' the wold falls to the pitiless bronze.

                        Man-travail and woman-war here we see enacted are.

                        When she and he beside the settle, he and she between the trestle-struts, mime the bitter dance to come.

Cheek by chin at the childer-crock where the quick tears drop

and the quick laughter dries the tears, within the rim of the shared curd⁄cup each fore⁄reads the world⁄storm.
Till the spoil⁄sport gammers sigh:

Now come on now little children, come on now it's past the hour. Sun's to roost, brood's in pent, dusk⁄star tops mound, lupa sniffs the lode⁄damps for stragglers late to byre.
Come now it's time to come now for tarry awhile and slow
cot's best for yeanlings
crib's best for babes
here's a rush to light you to bed
here's a fleece to cover your head
against the world⁄storm
brother by sister
under one *brethyn*
kith of the kin warmed at the one hearth⁄flame
(of the seed of far⁄gaffer? fair gammer's wer⁄gifts?)
cribbed in garth that the garth⁄Jill wards.

Though she inclines with attention from far fair⁄height outside all boundaries, beyond the known and kindly nomenclatures, where all names are one name, where all stones of demarcation dance and interchange, troia the skipping mountains, nod recognitions.
As when on known⁄site ritual frolics keep bucolic interval at eves and divisions when they mark the inflexions of the year and conjugate with trope and turn the season's syntax, with beating feet, with wands and pentagons to spell out the Trisagion.

Who laud and magnify with made, mutable and beggarly elements the unmade immutable begettings and precessions of fair⁄height, with halting sequences and unresolved rhythms, search⁄ingly, with what's to hand, under the inconstant lights that hover world⁄flats, that bright by fit and start the tangle of world⁄wood, rifting the dark drifts for the wanderers that wind the world⁄

meander, who seek hidden grammar to give back anathema its
first benignity.
Gathering all things in, twining each bruised stem to the swaying
trellis of the dance, the dance about the sawn lode⁄stake on the
hill where the hidden stillness is at the core of struggle, the dance
around the green lode⁄tree on far fair⁄height where the secret
guerdons hang and the bright prizes nod, where sits the queen
im Rosenhage eating the honey⁄cake, where the king sits, counting⁄
out his man⁄geld, rhyming the audits of all the world⁄holdings.

Where the marauder leaps the wall and the wall dances to the
marauder's leaping, where the plunging wolf⁄spear and the wolf's
pierced diaphragm sing the same song . . .

Yet, when she stoops to hear you children cry
                from the scattered and single habitations
or from the nucleated holdings
                from tower'd *castra*
                paved *civitas*
                treble⁄ramped *caer*
                or wattled *tref*
                        stockaded *gorod* or
                        trenched *burh*
from which ever child⁄crib within whatever enclosure
demarked by a dynast or staked by consent
wherever in which of the wide world⁄ridings
                you must not call her but by that name
which accords to the morphology of that place.
Now pray now little children for us all now, pray our gammer's
prayer according to our *disciplina* given to us
within our labyrinth on our dark mountain.
                Say now little children:
Sweet Jill of our hill hear us
bring slow bones safe at the lode⁄ford
keep lupa's bite without our wattles
make her bark keep children good

save us all from dux of far folk
save us from the men who plan.
Now sleep on, little children, sleep on now, while I tell out the
greater suffrages, not yet for young heads to understand:

Queen of the differentiated sites, administratrix of the demarcations, let our cry come unto you.
                  In all times of imperium save us when the
mercatores come save us
            from the guile of the *negotiatores* save us from the *missi*,
from the agents
           who think no shame
by inquest to audit what is shameful to tell
                 deliver us.
When they check their capitularies in their curias
                confuse their reckonings.
When they narrowly assess the *trefydd*
              by hide and rod
              by *pentan* and pent
by impost and fee on beast-head
              and roof-tree
and number the souls of men
              notch their tallies false
disorder what they have collated.
When they proscribe the diverse uses and impose the
rootless uniformities, pray for us.
            When they sit in *Consilium*
to liquidate the holy diversities
            mother of particular perfections
            queen of otherness
            mistress of asymmetry
patroness of things counter, parti, pied, several
protectress of things known and handled
help of things familiar and small
            wardress of the secret crevices
            of things wrapped and hidden
mediatrix of all the deposits

margravine of the troia
empress of the labyrinth
receive our prayers.
When they escheat to the Ram
in the Ram's curia
the seisin where the naiad sings
above where the forked rod bends
or where the dark outcrop
tells on the hidden seam
pray for the green valley.
When they come with writs of oyer and terminer
to hear the false and
determine the evil
according to the advices of the Ram's magnates who serve the
Ram's wife, who write in the Ram's book of Death.
In the bland megalopolitan light
where no shadow is by day or by night
be our shadow.
Remember the mound-kin, the kith of the *tarren* gone from this
mountain because of the exorbitance of the Ram . . . remember
them in the rectangular tenements, in the houses of the engines
that fabricate the ingenuities of the Ram . . . Mother of Flowers
save them then where no flower blows.
Though they shall not come again
because of the requirements of the Ram with respect to the world
plan, remember them where the dead forms multiply, where no
stamen leans, where the carried pollen falls to the adamant surfaces,
where is no crevice.
In all times of *Gleichschaltung*, in the days of the central economies,
set up the hedges of illusion round some remnant of us, twine the
wattles of mist, white-web a Gwydion-hedge
like fog on the *bryniau*
against the commissioners
and assessors bearing the writs of the Ram to square the world-
floor and number the tribes and write down the secret things and
take away the diversities by which we are, by which we call on
your name, sweet Jill of the demarcations
arc of differences

                    tower of individuation
                    queen of the minivers
        laughing in the mantle of variety
        belle of the mound
                              for Jac o'the mound
        our belle and donnabelle
                              on all the world⁄mountain.
In the December of our culture ward somewhere the secret seed,
under the mountain, under and between, between the grids of
the Ram's survey when he squares the world⁄circle.
Sweet Mair devise a mazy⁄guard
in and out and round about
double⁄dance defences
countermure and echelon meanders round
the holy mound
                    fence within the fence
pile the dun ash for the bright seed
              (within the curtained wood the canister
within the canister the budding rod)
troia in depth the shifting wattles of illusion for the ancilia for the
palladia for the kept memorials, because of the commissioners
of the Ram and the Ram's decree concerning the utility of the
hidden things.

When the technicians manipulate the dead limbs of our culture
as though it yet had life, have mercy on us. Open unto us, let us
enter a second time within your stola⁄folds in those days –
ventricle and refuge both, *hendref* for world⁄winter, asylum from
world⁄storm. Womb of the Lamb the spoiler of the Ram.

                              c. *1960 incorporating passages written earlier.*

Vernon Watkins provided a glossary of certain Welsh words in this poem:

brethyn	cloth	*tarren*	tump, knoll
bryniau	hills	*tref*	hamlet
caer	fort, castle, city	*trefydd*	hamlets
hendref	ancestral dwelling, winter quarters	*troia*	meander, from *troi*, to turn, and Troea, Troy.
pentan	hob, fire⁄stone		

64

THE HUNT

          . . . and the hundreds and twenties
of horsed *palatini*
          (to each *comitatus*
one Penteulu)
          that closely hedge
          with a wattle of weapons
the firsts among equals
          from the wattled *palasau*
the torqued *arglwyddi*
          of calamitous jealousy[1]
(if there were riders from the Faithful Fetter-locked War-Band
there were riders also from the Three Faithless War-Bands: the
riders who receive the shaft-shock
          in place of their radiant lords
the riders who slip the column
          whose lords alone
          receive the shafts)[2]
      when the men of proud spirit and the men of mean spirit, the
named and the unnamed of the Island and the name-bearing
steeds of the Island and the dogs of the Island and the silent lords
and the lords of loud mouth, the leaders of familiar visage from
the dear known-sites and the adjuvant stranger lords with aid for
the hog-hunt from over the Sleeve[3]

---

[1] The words *palatini*, Penteulu, *arglwyddi*, and jealousy all rhyme. The word
palasau (palaces) is pronounced approximately pal-ass-eye, accent on the middle
syllable.
    The Penteulu was the term used for the Captain of the Guard of the horse-troop
which constituted the *comitatus* of a Welsh ruler. Pronounce pen-tye-lee, accent on
the middle syllable.
    Arglwyddi (lords) pronounce approximately arr-gloo-with-ee – stress accent on
penultimate syllable. Perhaps arg-glwith-ee conveys it better.
[2] This passage in brackets refers to certain incidents and persons (such as
Gronw the Radiant) mentioned in the Triads of the Three Faithful War-Bands
and the Three Unfaithful War-Bands of the Island of Britain.
[3] In the Culhwch narrative mention is made of aid coming from across the
Channel, and at Cardigan the hog kills *gwilenhin brenin freinc*. Gwilenhin, King of
France.

and the wand-bearing lords that are kin to Fferyllt[1] (who learned from the Sibyl the Change Date and the Turn of Time) the lords who ride after deep consideration and the lords whose inveterate habit is to ride the riders who ride from interior compulsion and the riders who fear the narrow glances of the kindred.

Those who would stay for the dung-bailiff's daughter and those who would ride though the shining *matres* three by three sought to stay them.[2]

The riders who would mount though the green wound unstitched and those who would leave their mounts in stall if the bite of a gadfly could excuse them.

The innate Combroges,[3] by father by mother without mixed without brok'n without mean descent, all the lords from among the co-equals and the quasi-free of limited privilege, whose insult price is unequal but whose limb-price is equal for all the disproportion as to comeliness and power because the dignity belonging to the white limbs and innate in the shining members, annuls inequality of status and disallows distinctions of appearance.[4]

When the free and the bond and the mountain mares and the settled horses and the four-penny curs and the hounds of status in the wide, jewelled collars

when all the shining Arya[5] rode

[1] Fferyllt or Ffcryll is the Welsh form of the name Vergil. Pronounce approximately, fair-rillt. Owing to the medieval association of Vergil with prophetic and magical powers, any alchemist was called *fferyllt* and later the word became used of any chemist.

[2] The term *maer biswail*, 'dung bailiff', was used of the overseer of the villeins who worked on the court farmlands, thus making the jocular distinction between him and the Maer (from Lat. *maior*) of the province, an important executive official.

The 'shining *matres*, three by three' refers to a possible connection between the female cult-figures sculptured in groups of three of Romano-Celtic Antiquity, called *Deae Matres* and the term *Y Mamau*, The Mothers, used of the fairies in some parts of Wales.

[3] Combroges (pronounce com-bro-gees, accent on middle syllable), 'men of the same *patria*' from which word, Cymry, the Welsh people, derives. Compare Allobroges a people of Savoy mentioned by Classical writers and glossed as meaning 'men of a different *patria*'.

[4] This passage refers to various complex distinctions listed in the code known as 'The Laws of Hywel Dda'.

[5] The word Arya means the nobles or high-men, and has nothing whatever to do with race. Among the Sumerians, Chinese, Mongols and the Hamitic tribes of

with the diademed leader
                who directs the toil
                whose face is furrowed
with the weight of the enterprise
    the lord of the conspicious scars whose visage is fouled with
the hog⁄spittle whose cheeks are fretted with the grime of the
hunt⁄toil:
                if his forehead is radiant
like the smooth hill in the lateral light
                it is corrugated
like the defences of the hill
                because of his care for the land
and for the men of the land.
    If his eyes are narrowed for the stress of the hunt and because
of the hog they are moist for the ruin and for love of the recumbent
bodies that strew the ruin.
    If his embroidered habit is clearly from a palace wardrobe it
is mired and rent and his bruised limbs gleam from between the
rents, by reason of the excessive fury of his riding when he rode
the close thicket as though it were an open launde
                (indeed, was it he riding the forest⁄ride
or was the tangled forest riding?)
    for the thorns and flowers of the forest and the bright elm⁄
shoots and the twisted tanglewood of stamen and stem clung and
meshed him and starred him with variety
    and the green tendrils gartered him and briary⁄loops galloon
him with splinter⁄spike and broken blossom twining his royal
needlework
                and ruby petal⁄points counter
the countless points of his wounds
    and from his lifted cranium where the priced tresses dragged
with sweat stray his straight brow⁄furrows under the twisted
diadem

Africa, wherever there was a warrior⁄culture and the cult of the sky⁄god, the tribal
king or chieftain tended to personify that god, and be addressed by the same title.
As noted by Mr Christopher Dawson in *The Age of the Gods*, in the case of the
Etruscans a whole mixed people are known to history as 'the Lords', merely because
their female cult⁄figure was Turan, The Lady, and their male cult⁄figure Maristuran,
Mars the Lord.

to the numbered bones

of his scarred feet

and from the saturated forelock

of his maned mare

to her streaming flanks
and in broken festoons for her quivering fetlocks
he was caparison'd in the flora

of the woodlands of Britain

and like a stricken numen of the woods

he rode

with the trophies of the woods

upon him

who rode

for the healing of the woods

and because of the hog.

Like the breast of the cock⁄thrush that is torn in the hedge⁄
war when bright on the native mottle the deeper mottling is and
brighting the diversity of textures and crystal⁄bright on the
delicate fret the clear dew⁄drops gleam: so was his dappling and
his dreadful variety

the speckled lord of Prydain

in his twice⁄embroidered coat

the bleeding man in the green

and if through the trellis of green

and between the rents of the needlework

the whiteness of his body shone

so did his dark wounds glisten.

And if his eyes, from their scrutiny of the hog⁄track and from
considering the hog, turned to consider the men of the host (so
that the eyes of the men of the host met his eyes) it would be
difficult to speak of so extreme a metamorphosis.

When they paused at the check

when they drew breath.

And the sweat of the men of the host and of the horses salted
the dew of the forest⁄floor and the hard⁄breathing of the many
men and of the many dogs and of the horses woke the fauna⁄cry

of the Great Forest[1] and shook the silent flora.
     And the extremity of anger
alternating with sorrow
     on the furrowed faces
of the Arya
     transmogrified the calm face
of the morning
     as when the change-wind stirs
and the colours change in the boding thunder-calm
     because this was the Day
of the Passion of the Men of Britain
     when they hunted the Hog
life for life.

    c. 1964 incorporating passages written c. 1950 or earlier.

[1] The initial letters are in capitals because the reference is not only to a large tract of forest-land but to a district name, Fforest Fawr, an upland area of Breconshire which formed part of the itinerary taken by the boar, Trwyth, and Arthur's hunt.
 Note: This fragment is part of an incomplete attempt based on the native Welsh early medieval prose-tale, Culhwch ac Olwen, in which the predominant theme becomes the great hunt across the whole of southern Wales of the boar Trwyth by all the war-bands of the Island led by Arthur.

THE SLEEPING LORD

A brief note with regard to this fragment called provisionally 'The Sleeping Lord' is, for the following reasons, necessary. First, as here printed, various of its passages are subject to revision and there are certain other passages that I had hoped to include, but have excluded, partly on account of length and partly because I have not, for unforeseen reasons, been able to get them into the shape I wished in time for publication.

Secondly, it chances to be a piece that is essentially for the ear rather than the eye. It chances also that owing to its subject matter it contains a number of words, mainly proper and common nouns, in Welsh. This in turn, has made it necessary to try to convey some approximate idea of the sound of those words.

For example, should the reader not know, that the Welsh 'au' in, say, 'mamau' (mothers) is similar in sound to the terminating syllable in the English words 'lullaby' or 'magpie', or the Latin word 'puellae', then the whole feeling of the sentence in which those words were in juxta-position would be lost. I have therefore been compelled to append a number of the sounds of such Welsh terms as I had to use in order to evoke the feel and ethos inherent in the 'materia' or subject matter.

Here I must apologize to Welsh readers for these inadequate and elementary attempts. I fully realize that the approximations are extremely arbitrary and in some cases may be wide of the mark, but something of the sort had to be attempted and had to be as brief as possible. I have given the Welsh diphthongs 'ae, ai, au, ei' and 'eu' as approximating more or less to the English 'ei' in 'height', whereas in fact these diphthongs vary. In a few cases I gave the English word 'eye' as corresponding to the Welsh 'au'. For one of the two sounds of the Welsh 'y' I give 'uh' as in the English 'u' in run, so that 'Y Forwyn' (The Virgin) is given as being pronounced uh vôr-win.

I have excluded all other notes from this version, except in a few instances.

And is his bed wide

        is his bed deep on the folded strata

is his bed long

        where is his bed and
        where has he lain him

from north of Llanfair‑ym‑Muallt

        (a name of double *gladius*‑piercings)[1]

south to the carboniferous vaultings of Gŵyr[2]

        (where in the sea‑slope chamber

they shovelled aside the shards & breccia

        the domestic litter and man‑squalor

of gnawed marrowbones and hearth‑ash
with utile shovels fashioned of clavicle‑bones

        of warm‑felled great fauna.

Donated the life‑signa:

        the crocked viatic meal
        the flint‑worked ivory agalma

the sacral sea‑shell trinkets

        posited with care the vivific amulets

of gleam‑white rodded ivory

        and, with oxide of iron

ochred life‑red the cerements

        of the strong limbs

of the young *nobilis*

        the first of the sleepers of

Pritenia, *pars dextralis*, O! aeons & aeons

        before we were insular'd.)

Is the tump by Honddu[3]

        his lifted bolster?
        does a gritstone outcrop

incommode him?

[1] Llanfair‑ym‑Muallt: 'Mary's church in Buellt'. The town now called Builth Wells. It was between Llanfair and Llanganten that the Lord Llywelyn, Prince of Wales was killed in 1282. Hence my reference to a *double* piercing in that any place‑ name with Marian associations necessarily recalls the passage in the gospel of the *gladius* that would pierce the heart of the God‑bearer. Pronounce: llan‑veir‑um‑ mee‑allt.

[2] Gŵyr: The Gower Peninsular; pronounce approximately goo‑eer. It was in Gŵyr that human remains, ritually buried, were discovered of a young man of the Palaeolithic period, so many, many millenniums prior to Britain becoming an island.

[3] Honddu: pronounce hón‑thee.

                    does a deep syncline
                    sag beneath him?
or does his dinted thorax rest
                         where the contorted heights
                         themselves rest
on a lateral pressured anticline?
Does his russet-hued mattress
                         does his rug of shaly grey
ease at all for his royal dorsals
                         the faulted under-bedding.
Augite-hard and very chill
                         do scattered *cerrig*[1]
jutt to discomfort him?
                         Millenniums on millennia since
this cold scoria dyked up molten
when the sedimented, slowly layered strata
(so great the slow heaped labour of their conditor
the patient creature of water) said each to each other:
'There's no resisting here:
                    the Word if made Fire.'

    If his strong spine rest
                    on the bald heights
where, would you say, does his Foot-Holder kneel?
In what deep vale
                    does this fidell official
ward this lord's Achilles' heel?
                    Does he lap
the bruised *daudroed*[2] of his lord
and watch lest harm should befall the lord's person (which is all
that is expressly demanded of a *troed*[3]-holder) or over and above
what is of obligation does he do what is his to do with some
measure of the dedication of the daughter of Pebin of the Water-
Meadow, who held in her lap the two feet of the shape-shifting

---

[1] *cerrig*: stones; pronounce ker-rig 'er' as in errand.
[2] *daudroed*: two feet; (*dau*, two, + troed, foot). Pronounce approximately die-droid.
[3] *troed*: foot; pronounce troid.

Rhi[1] of Arfon?[2]
Or, silently, attentively & carefully
        and with latreutic veneration   *Latreuein Gk*
                                  to serve
as did Mair Modlen[3]
the eternally pierced feet
        of the Shepherd of Greekland
        the Heofon-Cyning
born of Y Forwyn Fair[4]
        lapped in hay in the ox's stall
next the grey ass in the caved *stabulum*
ad praesepem in heye Bedlem
        that is bothe bryht and schen.

Does he lean low to his high office
        in the leafy hollow
        below the bare *rhiw*[5]
where the sparse hill-flora
        begins to thicken
by the rushing *nant*[6] where the elders grow
and the talled-stemmed *ffion*[7]
        put on the purple
to outbright the green gossamer fronds
of the spume-born maiden's hair.

    It were wise to not bruise nor fracture
by whatever inadvertence, these delicate agalma
for of such are the things
        made over to her.

Where, too, would you guess

  [1] Rhi: King; pronounce rhee, 'r' trilled, 'h' very aspirated.

  [2] Arfon: pronounce arr-von.

  [3] Mair Modlen: Mary Magdelen. Pronounce approximately meirr (ei as in height) mód-len.

  [4] Y Forwyn Fair: The Virgin Mary; mutated forms of *morwyn*, maiden and Mair, Mary; pronounce approximately uh vór-win veir (ei as in height, each 'r' trilled).

  [5] *rhiw*: a hill-slope; pronounce, rhee-oo.

  [6] *nant*: a small stream.

  [7] *ffion*: foxgloves; pronounce fee-on.

                    might his Candle⁄bearer be standing
to hold and ward
                    against the rising valley⁄*wynt*[1]
his iron⁄spiked guttering light
                    The twisted flax⁄wick
                    (without which calcined death
no uprising, warm, gold⁄rayed *cannwyll*[2]⁄life)
                    bends one way
with the wind⁄bowed elder boughs
and the pliant bending of the wild elm
                    (that serves well the bowyers)
and the resistant limbs
                    of the tough, gnarled *derwen*[3] even
lean all to the swaying briary⁄tangle
that shelters low
                    in the deeps of the valley⁄wood
the fragile *blodyn⁄y⁄gwynt*[4]

    And the wind⁄gusts do not slacken
but buffet stronger and more chill
                    as the dusk deepens
over the high *gwaundir*[5]
                    and below in the *glynnoedd*[6]
where the *nentydd*[7] run
                    to conflow with the *afon*[8]
where too is the running of the deer

---

    [1] *wynt* mutation of *gwynt*, wind; pronounce wint.

    [2] *cannwyll*: from Latin *candela*. Pronounce approximately cánooill; the double 'll' representing the Welsh *ll* for which there is no corresponding sound in English.

    [3] *derwen*: an oak tree; pronounce dér⁄wen, the *er* of the accented syllable is like the 'er' in derelict or errand.

    [4] *blodyn⁄y⁄gwynt*: flower of the wind or wood⁄anemone; pronounce blod⁄din⁄uh⁄gwint.

    [5] *gwaundir*: moorland; *gwaun*, moor *tir*, land. Pronounce very approximately gwein ('ei' as in height) deerr.

    [6] *glynnoed*: plural of *glyn*, glen. Pronounce glún⁄noithe.

    [7] *nentydd*: plural of *nant*, a brook. Pronounce approximately nentith, 'th' as in breathe.

    [8] *afon*: river; pronounce áv⁄von.

whose desire is toward these water‑brooks.

Over the whole terrain
                    and the denizens of the terrain
the darking pall falls
                    and the chill wind rises higher.

    Is the season sequence out of joint
                    that leafy boughs should tremor so
for a night‑fall gust
                    at this age of the solar year
scarcely descendent as yet
                    from the apex‑house
of the shining Twin‑Brothers of
                    Helen the Wall?
Be that as may
                    by whatever freak of nature
or by the widdershin spell
                    of a wand‑waver
this night‑wind of the temperate Ides of Quintilis
blows half a gale & boreal at that.
                    Indeed, so chill it is
it strikes to the bone, more like the wind
                    of the lengthening light
                    of the strengthening cold
of round or about
                    the Ides of the mensis of Janus
when the wintry Sol has turned his back
                    to the heavenly thack of The Hoedus
and, coursing through the bleaker house of The‑Man‑that‑Pours‑
the‑Water‑Out, careens on his fixed and predetermined cursus,
with the axle‑tree of his essedum upward steeved, under the
icicled roof of the februal house of The‑Fish‑with‑the‑Glistening‑
Tails, when, still on the climb, he has, in part, his cours y‑ronne
in the martial house of Aries whose blast is through with a
battering drive the thickest *pexa* of closest weave, and Mavors'

petrabula (artfully virid is their camouflage) are brought to bear
for his barrage of steelcold stones of hail
                              which pelting of this pittiless storme
makes the stripped but green‑budding boughs
moan and complain afresh to each other
yn y gaeaf oer.[1]

But whatever may have been the cause of this phenomenon
and altogether irrespective of it and apart too from what is
required and codified in the Notitia of degrees & precedence
touching the precise duties of a lord's candle‑bearer and as to
where and when he must stand in the lord's *neuadd,*[2] it is the most
likely thing in the world that you will, none the less, find him
here, on the open *mynnydd‑dir*[3]

for it is his innate habit to be wherever his lord is unless pre‑
vented by violence or by one of the lord's chief officers, for he is
listed last on the roster of the named functionaries attendant upon
the lord and is accounted least among them: what is he compared
with the Chief Huntsman let alone the Chief Falconer or the
Bard of the Household? And as for the Justiciar or the Maer of
the Palace,[4] compared with these he is nothing
                              yet is he not the Light‑Bearer?
whose but his the inalienable privilege
                              to hold upright
                              before the Bear of the Island
in his timber‑pillar'd hall

AGGER
= MOUND
CINCTURE
= Circled

(which stands within the agger‑cinctured *maenol*[5]) the tall, taper‑
ing, flax‑cored candela of pure wax (the natural produce of the
creatures labouring in the royal hives but made a true artefact by
the best chandlers of the royal *maenol*)

[1] *yn y gaeaf oer*: in the winter cold. Pronounce approximately un uh gúy‑av oirr.
[2] *neuadd*: hall; pronounce approximately nye‑ath, 'th' as in breathe.
[3] *mynnydd‑dir*: mountain‑land. Pronounce mún‑nith ('th' as in breathe) deerr.
[4] Maer: from Latin *maior*, The Mayor of the Palace. Pronounce very approxi‑
mately meir, 'ei' as in height.
[5] *maenol*: the whole area of the lord's *llys* or court, in which the *neuadd* or hall
stands. Pronounce approximately mein ('ei' as height) nol.

that flames upward
in perfection of form
                        like the leaf-shaped war-heads
that gleam from the long-hafted spears
                        of the lord's body-guard
but immeasurably greater
                        is the pulchritude
for the quivering gleam of it
is of living light
                        and light
(so these *clerigwyr*[1] argue)
                        is, in itself, a good
ergo, should this *candela*-bearer
                        presume so far as to argue that
his *cannwyll* does indeed constitute
One of the Three Primary Signa
                        of the Son of Mary
. . . *unig-anedig Fab Duw*[2]
                        . . . *ante omnia saecula*
lumen de lumine . . .
                        by whom all things . . .
who should blame him?

So whether his lord is in hall or on circuit of the land, he's most like to be about somewhere, you can count on that.

Whether seated
                        at his board on the dais wearing such
insignia as is proper for him, his head circled with the pale-bright
talaith[3] of hammered-thin river-gold, his thinning tawny hair of

---

[1] *clerigwyr*: clerks, clerics; Pronounce approximately cler-rig-weir.
[2] *unig-anedig Fab Duw*: only-begotten Son of God; pronounce approximately in-ig an-nédig vahb dee-oo.
[3] *talaith*: diadem, circlet, coronet. Pronounce approximately tál-eith, 'ei' as in height.

lost lustre streaked whitish straying his brows' deep-dug care-
furrows

          (for *long* has he been the Director of Toil,
the strategos bearing the weight of the defence-struggle on three
fronts and the heavier weight of the treason-tangle of the sub-
reguli of equal privilege, the bane of the island)
when standing near him

          is the Priest of the Household
who must chant the *Pater*

          and offer the *bendith*[1]
when the knife has been put

          into the peppered meat
and drink has been put into the *cornu*

          and the Silentiary
has struck the post for the *pared*[2]

          to hear
and for all the men

          under the *gafl*[3] -treed roof-tree
of the *neuadd*, to hear
whether they are seated or standing

          on either side of the wattle-twined *cancelli*
below or above

          the centred hearth-stone
(where the life of the household smoulders)

          to hear
with his face toward the Arglwydd[4] and toward those about him,

[1] *bendith*: blessing.

[2] *pared*: screen or partition, from *parietem*. Pronounce approximately pá-red.
   The hall (*neuadd*) of a Welsh chieftain was of wooden construction. Wooden
pillars supported the roof-tree. It was partly divided into an 'upper' and a 'lower'
hall by two half screens running from the side walls, rather as a church is divided
into nave and chancel (*cancelli*). The fire (which must on no account go out, for it
represented the life of the household) was placed centrally between the two half
partitions. Each of the various officers of the court sat in order of precedence. The
Silentiary (*Gostegwr*) struck with his rod one of the supporting pillars when silence
was required. There is a Welsh proverbial saying about striking the post for the
partition to hear (*Taro'r post i 'r pared glywed*) which I presume, but do not know,
reflects this ancient construction of the halls of these rulers as described in the Welsh
Laws.

[3] *gafl*: fork. Pronounce approximately gáv-el.

[4] Arglwydd: Lord; pronounce approximately árr-glooith, 'th' as in breathe.

after he has said certain versicles, he begins the *bendith* proper, and with a slight inclination of his body toward the man that wears the golden fillet, he makes the life⁄sign over all the men in the smoked⁄wreathed *neuadd*, saying, in a clear voice:

Bene ✠ dic, Domine nos

and then, over the food⁄vessels, and

over the distilled, golden *meddlyn*[1]

in the drink vessels

over the red⁄gilt bowl

that holds the blood⁄red wine

(freighted from Bwrgwyn via Sabrina Aestuarium)

he makes the same signum, saying

et haec ✠ tua dona . . .

and when he comes to the words which in the other tongue of men of the Island signify *trwy Iesu Grist ein Harglwydd*[2] he bows his head and then, in silence, inly to himself and but for a brief moment, he makes memento of those who no longer require such as himself to bless their meat & drink, for elsewhere is their wide *maenol*

at least, such is his hope.

His silent, brief and momentary recalling is firstly of those Athletes of God, who in the waste⁄lands & deep wilds of the Island and on the spray⁄swept skerries and desolate *insulae* where the white⁄pinioned sea⁄birds nest, had sought out places of retreat and had made the White Oblation for the living and the dead in those solitudes, in the habitat of wolves and wild⁄cat and such like creatures of the Logos (by whom all creatures are that are) and his silent memento is next of those who had made the same *anamnesis* in the cities of the provinces of Britannia which the Survey had aligned according to the quadrilateral plan, *per scamna et strigas* and had determined the run of the *limes transversus* for masons to wall the auspicious area with squared stone, which cities are now either calcined heaps or, if standing intact, are desolate and deserted of people.

[1] *meddlyn*: mead; pronounce approximately meth ('th' as in breathe) lin.

[2] *trwy Iesu Grist ein Harglwydd*: through Jesus Christ our Lord; pronounce approximately troo⁄ee yéss⁄ee greest ine hárr⁄glooith, 'th' as in breathe, 'h' strongly aspirated.

Quomodo sedet sola civitas plena populo![1]

> How? Why?
> It is because of the long, long
>   and continuing power-struggle
> for the fair lands of Britain
>   and the ebb & flow of the devastation-
> waves of the war-bands
>   for no provinces of the West
> were longer contested than these provinces
>   nor is the end yet
>   for that tide rises higher
> nor can it now be stayed.

And next his recalling is of those who made the same Oblation in the hill-lands and valley-ways, labouring among a mixed folk of low and high estate, some more rapacious, maybe, than the creatures of the wilds, being savaged by much tribulation, up-rooted from various provinces, some come by thalassic routes from southern Gaul bringing with them a valuable leaven . . .

Or whether they offered the Eternal Victim within the wattled enclosures: *bangorau,*[2] *monasterii, clasordai*[3] where they live in common under the common rule of an *abad*[4] who may chance to be also the Antistita who alone is able to place upon any man the condition of being an Offerand. But once an *Offeiriad* always an *Offeiriad.* Nor does death affect this conditioning; for it is with the indelible marks of the priesthood of the Son of Mair upon him that he will, *yn Nydd o Farn,*[5] face the Son of Mair.

---

[1] See the First Lesson of the First Nocturn for Matins of Feria V in Coena Domini (Maundy Thursday) which begins '*Incipit Lamentatio Jeremiae Prophetae. Aleph: Quomodo sedet sola civitas plena populo*'.

[2] *bangorau*: plural of *bangor* in the sense of a wattled enclosure of religious. Pronounce approximately ban-gor-rei ('ei' as in height).

[3] *clasordai* (plural of *clasordy*): cloisters or monastic houses; pronounce approximately clas-órr-dei.

[4] *abad*: abbot, pronounce áb-bad. [5] *yn Nydd o Farn*: in the Day of Judgement.

Or whether they stood solitary at the *mensa* far from the next nearest *claswr*[1] in the little white *addoldy*[2] under the green elbow of the hill, which the chief man of that locality has caused to be twined of pliant saplings and lime washed without and within

or whether the merits of the same Victim are pleaded at the stone in the stone built *eglwys* (its gapped roofing repaired, more or less, with thatch, its broken walling patched with unmortared rubble) that stands by the narrowing and silted estuary where the great heaped ruins are, that tell of vanished wharves and emporia and cement bonded brick & dressed stone store cellae for bonded goods and where walk the ghosts of customs officials and where mildewed scraps of sight drafts, shards of tessera tallies and fragile as tinder fragmented papyri, that are wraiths of filed bills of lading, litter here and there the great sandstone blocks of fallen vaulting . . . where also, if you chance to be as lettered as the Irish eremite up stream, you can read, freely & lightly scratched in the plaster of a shattered pilaster, in *mercatores'* Greek, what seems to mean: Kallistratos loves Julia and so does Henben and so do I
and a bit more
that you can't decipher . . .

or whether the same anamnesis was made in the *capel freninol*,[3] within the ditched & guarded defences of a *caer* of a lord of the land
as here & now, in the Bear's chapel.

And next, his rapid memento is of those lords & rulers and men of name in the land in times past: *penmilwyr*,[4] *aergwn*,[5] *aergyfeddau*,[6] *cymdeithion yn y ffosydd*,[7] *cadfridogion*,[8] *tribuni militum*,

[1] *claswr*: man from or in a *clasordy*, a monastic or priest. Pronounce clás oorr.

[2] *addoldy*: place of worship. Pronounce approximately a thól dee, 'a' as in apple, 'th' as in those. [3] *capel freninol*: royal chapel. Pronounce cap el vren nin ol.

[4] *penmilwyr*: commander of soldiers. Pronounce approximately pen míl weir.

[5] *aergwn*: warriors, lit. dogs of battle. Pronounce eir goon.

[6] *aergyfeddau*: battle comrades. Pronounce approximately eir guv véth ei, 'th' as in breathe, 'ei' as in height.

[7] *cymdeithion yn y ffosydd*: companions in the defences or *fossae*. Pronounce very approximately cum deith ee on un uh foss sith, final 'th' as in breathe.

[8] *cadfridogion*: generals. Pronounce cad vrid óg ee on.

pennaethau,[1] *comitates, rhiau*,[2] *cadflaenoriaid*,[3] *sub-reguli,* pendragons, *protectores, rhaglawiaid*,[4] *strategoi, duces,* saviours & leaders of varying eminence together with *gwyr o galon*[5] of all sorts. Some but recent, others far, far, far back: such as Belinos of whom the Bard of the Household claimed to have some arcane tradition. About which, he, himself, the Priest of the Household, thought of uncertain authenticity; but, to say the truth, he was dubious of much that these poets asserted though they were indeed most skilled artists and remembrancers & conservators of the things of the Island, yet he suspected that they tended to be weavers also of the fabulous and were men over-jealous of their status and secretive touching their *traditio,* but then, after all, their *disciplina* was other than his and this he knew for certain that whatever else they were, they were men who loved the things of the Island, and so did he.

Then there was Cunobelinos the Radiant of whom he fancied he had himself found some mention in a Latin *historia,* but he could no longer at all recollect by what author – perhaps he had merely imagined it, which worried him; but he had in his younger years read in various works the names of which he could barely recall; but there was Eusebius, Orosius, Venantius, Prosper, apart from fragments, at all events, of both Greek and Latin authors of very great fame, *cyn Cred,*[6] and there was Martianus Capella and Faustus called 'of Regensium' because he had been consecrated *esgob*[7] to that place, but he was a man of this Island who had written well touching the Victim of the Offering. But now that he was many winters old, the diverse nature of what he had read had become sadly intermeddled and

[1] *pennaethau*: chieftains. Pronounce approximately pen-eíth-ei; 'ei' as in height.
[2] *rhiau*: kings. Pronounce approximately rhée-ei 'ei' as in height.
[3] *cadflaenoriaid*: leaders in battle Pronounce approximately cad-vlein-órr-ee-eid ('ei' as in height).
[4] *rhaglawiaid*: governors of districts. Pronounce approximately rhag-láu-ee-eid. The accented syllable rhymes with 'vow', 'ei' as in height.
[5] *gwyr o galon*: men of valour (lit. men of heart). Pronounce approximately goo-eér o gál-on.
[6] *cyn Cred*: B.C. lit. 'before the Creed'. Pronounce approximately kin kraid.
[7] *esgob*: *epsicopus*. Pronounce éss-gob.

very greatly confused. But anyway his main concern was with
Yr Efengyl Lan[1] and he liked to dwell on the thought that the
word *efengyl* (owing, he supposed, to the kiss given at that part of
the Oblation called the *pax*) could, in the tongue of his country-
men, mean a kiss. For what, after all, is the Hagion Evangelion
if not the salutation or kiss of the eternally begotten Logos? And
how could that salutation have been possible but for the pliancy
of Mary & her *fiat mihi?* Which is why Irenaeus had written that
this *puella*, Mair Wenfydedig,[2] was 'constituted the cause of our
salvation'. Now this Irenaeus, away back, five or more long life-
times back, in the days of his great-great-great grandfathers or
beyond again, when the Ymherawdr[3] Aurelius, an able enough
ruler, but much given to fine thoughts, high-flown principles,
moralizings and the like (a type for which he had little use – he
much preferred such as the Captain of the Guard) had, either by
various *mandata* or by direct Imperial Edict, caused great harm
to the *plebs Xti* and had made it perilous for the priesthood of
Melchisedec to offer the Oblation for the living & the dead –
anyhow, during that time, Irenaeus was an *esgob* in Gallia
Lugdunensis, but had come there from the coast of Ionia in Asia
(not very far from Galatia where there are men that speak the
same tongue as the men of the Island) and this Irenaeus had known
the holy man Polycarp who in turn had known Ieuan Cariadusaf[4] to whom had been committed the care & safeguarding of
Mair the Mother by the direct mandate of the Incarnate Logos,
even when he was reigning from the terrible stauros, his only
purple his golden blood-flow

shed PRO VOBIS ET PRO MULTIS

consummating in the unlit noon-dark

on Moel-y-Penglog[5]

the Oblation made at the lighted feast board.

[1] Yr Efengyl Lan: The Holy Gospel. Pronounce approximately ur eh-veng-il
lahn.
[2] Mair Wenfydedig: Blessed Mary. Pronounce approximately meirr ('ei' as in
height) wen-vud-déd-ig.
[3] Ymherawdr: *Imperator*. Pronounce approximately um-her-row-der.
[4] Ieuan Cariadusaf: John the Most Beloved. Pronounce very approximately yei-
an ca-ree-ad-iss-av.
[5] Moel-y-Penglog: 'Skull-Hill' Pronounce moil uh pen-glog.

Hence what the ecclesia holds touching this *puella*, Mair, is, as stated by Irenaeus, of extra weight, seeing that his *traditio* was received so directly from Polycarp Hên,[1] the Antistita of Smyrna who had known and talked with the beloved Johannes, that the men of the Island call Ieuan or Ioan.[2]

And when he considered the four-fold account in the books of the *quattuor evangelia* he thought what are these if not a kind of Pedair Cainc y Mabinogi[3] *sanctaidd?*[4] in that they proclaim the true mabinogi of the Maban[5] the Pantocrator and of the veritable mother of anxiety, the Rhiannon[6] who is indeed the ever glorious Theotokos yet Queen of Sorrows and *gladius* pierced – what better, he thinks, than that this four-fold marvel-tale should be called The Tale of the Kiss of the Son of Mair?

Then there was the Blessed Bran of whom the tale-tellers tell a most wondrous tale and then the names of men more prosaic but more credible to him: Paternus of the Red Pexa, Cunedda Wledig[7] the Conditor and, far more recent and so more green in the memory, the Count Ambrosius Aurelianus that men call Emrys Wledig, associated, by some, with the eastern defences called the Maritime Tract and Aircol Hîr[8] and his line, *protectores* of Demetia in the west . . . and many, many, many more whose bones lie under the green mounds of the Island; nor in his rapid memento of these many, did he forget the golden torqued *puellae* of gentle nurture, *arglwyddesau*,[9] *matronae* and *breninesau*[10] who, in

[1] Polycarp Hên: Old Polycarp. The long Welsh *e* in *bên* is more or less as the 'a' in lane or bane, but is a pure vowel.

[2] Ioan: pronounce very approximately yó-an, as said it's one syllable.

[3] Pedair Cainc y Mabinogi: The Four Branches of the Mabinogi. Pronounce approximately péd-eir-keink uh mab-in-óg-ee.

[4] *sanctaidd* holy, sacred. Pronounce approximately sank-teithe.

[5] Maban: a man-child, but here reflecting Mabon or Maponos the Celtic cult-figure the Son of Modron, the Mother-figure. Pronounce máb-an.

[6] Rhiannon: 'The Great Queen'. Pronounce rhee-án-non.

[7] Cunedda Wledig: pronounce approximately kin-eth-ah ('th' as in breathe) oo-léd-ig.

[8] Aircol Hîr: pronounce approximately íre-col heer. Agricola the Tall.

[9] *arglwyddesau*: the plural of *arglwyddes*, the wife of a lord. Pronounce approximately arr-glooith-és-eye, ('th' as in breathe).

[10] *breninesau*: queens. Pronounce approximately bren-nin-és-eye.
Thus both these words rhyme with *matronae* and *puellae*.

their life-days, had sustained the men of the Island, but whose bodies lie as hers for whom was digged the square grave on Alaw[1]-bank in Mona Insula, and Creiddylad[2] the daughter of Lear than whom no maiden of the Island or of the isles in the waters that moat the Island could compare in majesty either in her life-time or in the ages before her or in the times yet to be; and Elen[3] the daughter of Coil, lord of Stratha Clauda between the Vallum & the Wall and there was she whose agnomen was Aurfron[4] on account, it would appear, of her numinous & shining virtue, for the epithet 'golden' betokens what is not patient of tarnish . . .

and there were Slendernecks and Fairnecks and she that was called Bright Day, the daughter of the *gwledig*,[5] Amlawdd (of whom some rumour that he was a *princeps* from over the Sea of Cronos, yn Nenmarc, owing, he supposed, to a complex tangle of like-sounding *nomina*, for according to the genealogies he was a man of this Island and a son of Cunedda Wledig) & there was the lovely Gwenlliant,[6] who though her beauty was indeed great, yet was she named by the men of the Island Y Forwyn Fawr-frydig,[7] because the shining virtue called *megalopsychia*, the most prized of the virtues, exceeded even her outward splendour of form . . .

and many, many more whose names are, for whatever reason, on the diptycha of the Island; and vastly many more still, whether men or womenkind, of neither fame nor recorded *nomen*, whether bond or freed or innately free, of far back or of but recent decease, whose burial mounds are known or unknown or for whom no mound was ever raised or any mark set up of even the meanest sort to show the site of their interment; or those whose white bodies

[1] Alaw, rhymes with 'vow', accent on the first syllable.
[2] Creiddylad: pronounce approximately crei-thúl-ad, 'th' in as breathe.
[3] Elen: pronounce él-en.
[4] Aurfron: Golden Breast. Pronounce approximately eir ('ei' as in height) vron.
[5] *gwledig*: ruler. Pronounce approximately goo-léd-ig.
[6] Gwenlliant: pronounce approximately gwen-llee-ant (stress on the second syllable).
[7] Y Forwyn Fawrfrydig: The Magnanimous Maiden. Pronounce approximately uh vor-win vowr-vrúd-ig.

were shovelled into earth in haste, without funerary rites of any sort whatever; or those – a very, very great number, whose bodies, whether stripped naked or in full battle-gear were left to be the raven's gain and supper for the hovering kite and for the black-nebbed corbie that waits the *aerfor*[1]-ebb: the deeper the stillness of the *aerdawelwch*,[2] the higher heaped the banquet that she loves.

For these and for all the departed of the Island and indeed not only for those of the Island of the Mighty, nor only for those of the Patriarchate of the West, nor yet only for the departed of these provinces together with those of the provinces that are within the jurisdiction of the Patriarch whose seat is at Caergystennin[3]

> where Urbs is Polis

far side the narrowing *culfor*[4]

> that links Middle Sea

with Pontus Euxinus

> where the Ymherawdr[5]
> wearing his colobium sindonis

sits in the Sacred Palace

> but for the departed

of the entire universal orbis

from the unknown beginnings

> unguessed millenniums back

until now:

FOR THESE ALL

he makes his silent, secret

> devout and swift memento.

And discreetly and with scarcely any discernible movement he makes once again the salvific sign, saying less than half-audibly: *Requiem aeternam dona eis, Domine.*

But had he said these words never so low or had the slight movement of his right hand across the folds of his tunica been

---

[1] *aerfor*: tide of battle (*aer*, battle + *mor*, sea). Pronounce approximately eir-vor.

[2] *aerdawelwch*: silence after a battle (*aer* + *tawelwch*, stillness. Pronounce approximately eir-dou-wél-ooch 'dou' rhymes with 'vow'.

[3] Caergystennin: The fortress (or city) of Constantinus. Pronounce keir ('ei' as in height) gus-tén-nin.

[4] *culfor*: a confined sea-way. Pronounce kîl-vor.

[5] Ymherawdr: *Imperator*. Pronounce approximately um-her-rów-der.

even less than it was, the Candlebearer would have heard and seen; and though standing a good few paces from him, did hear and see, and, though the office of Cannwyllyd[1] gives him no right whatever to speak in the lord's hall, yet he could not contain himself, and though, the Lord Christ knows, he is not, by any means, a clerk, he sings out in a high, clear and distinct voice, the respond: *ET LUX PERPETUA LUCEAT EIS.*

So then, whether seated
               at this board in his hall
or lying on his sleep⁄board
               in his lime whited *ystafell*[2]
with his bed⁄coverlet over him to cover him
               a work of the Chief Stitching Maid
to Yr Arglwyddes[3] (his, the Bear's wife)
of many vairs of stitched together
               marten⁄cat pelts
contrived without visible seam
               from the top throughout.

               Or, here, out
on the cold, open *moelion*[4]
               his only coverlet
his madder⁄dyed war⁄*sagum*
               where he slumbers awhile
from the hunt⁄toil:
               carried lights
               for the lord

[1] Cannwyllyd: Candle⁄bearer. Pronounce approximately can⁄will⁄led,('ll' = Welsh *ll*).

[2] ystafell: chamber. Pronounce us⁄táv⁄ell. The word here refers to the private apartment of the lord and his wife within the *llys* or court. It derives from late⁄ Latin *stabellum*, a residence, and in the 9th century stanzas about the destruction of Cynddylan's court the word is used of the whole residence: *Stavell Gyndylan* in the original orthography.

[3] Yr Arglwyddes: the wife of the Arglwydd. Pronounce approximately ur ar⁄gloóith⁄ess, 'th' as in breathe.

[4] *moelion*: plural of *moel*, a bare hill. Pronounce approximately moil⁄ee⁄on.

in his pillar'd basilica

> carried lights
> for the lord

fain to lie down

> in the hog-wasted *blaendir*[1]

scorch-marks only

> where were the white dwellings:

stafell[2] of the lord of the Cantref

> *ys tywyll heno*

shieling of the *taeog*[3] from the bond-tref

> *heb dan, heb wely.*[4]

And the trees of the *llannerch?*[5]

> Why are they fallen?

What of the *llwyn*[6] where the fair *onnen*[7] grew and the silvery
queen of the *coedwig*[8] (as tough as she's graced & slender) that

---

[1] *blaendir*: borderland, but meaning also uplands, high hill-country that is also
a place of boundaries. Pronounce approximately blein ('ei' as in height) deerr.

[2] *stafell*: see note on the preceding page.

[3] *taeog*: a villein or man bound to the land. Pronounce approximately tei-og.

[4] *ys tywyll heno*: is dark tonight. Pronounce us tuh-will ('ll' represents Welsh *ll*)
hen-no, *heb dan, heb wely*: without fire, without bed. Pronounce approximately habe
dahn, habe wel-ee.

The use here of these two lines requires some explanation seeing that my knowledge of Welsh is so extremely scanty and that I have to rely in the main on transla-
tions. The lines quoted form part of one of the earliest fragments of Welsh poetry
and seem to me to incant and evoke so much that is central to a great tradition at
its strongest and most moving. They are part of a ninth century series of stanzas in
which the princess Heledd of Powys laments the death of her brother Cynddylan
and the destruction of his court at Pengwern (Shrewsbury) by the Angles. In the
older orthography the words of this stanza read

> Stavell Gyndylan ys tywyll heno
> heb dan, heb wely.

'The "hall" of Cynddylan is dark tonight, without fire without bed.' The words
Stavell Gyndylan are repeated as the opening words of each of the (sixteen) stanzas
so that they burn themselves into the mind, very much as do certain great phrases
that echo in a Liturgy, as for example, the words I have ventured to use earlier
from the Roman rite of *Tenebrae* 'How does the city sit solitary that was full of
people!' Such words, as with these of the princess Heledd have a permanacy and
evoke a whole situation far beyond their immediate 'meaning' that, in my view,
it is our duty to conserve them however little we 'know' the original languages.

[5] *llannerch*: a glade. Pronounce llan-nerch the 'er' as in errand.

[6] *llwyn*: a grove. Pronounce lloo-in.

[7] *onnen*: ash tree. Pronounce ón-nen.

[8] *coedwig*: a wood. Pronounce coid-wig.

88

whispers her secrets low to the divining hazel, and the resistant
oak boughs that antler'd dark above the hornbeam?

> *Incedunt arbusta per alta*
> *rapacibus caedunt*
> *Percellunt sacras quercus . . .*
> *Fraxinus frangitur . . .*[1]

Not by long-hafted whetted steel axe-blades
                    are these fallen
that graced the high slope
                    that green-filigreed
the green hollow
                    but by the riving tusks
of the great hog
                    are they felled.
It is the Boar Trwyth[2]
                    that has pierced through
the stout-fibred living wood
                    that bears the sacral bough of gold.
  It is the hog that has ravaged the fair *onnen* and the hornbeam
and the Queen of the Woods. It is the hog that has tusk-riven the

---

[1] *Incedunt arbusta . . .* Perhaps a note is necessary to indicate why I felt impelled
to make use of a few words from Ennius, *Annals* Bk. vi, descriptive of the felling
by woodmen's axes (*secures*) of the great spreading high trees which he apparently
had taken largely from Homer and which Vergil was to use in part from him, and
others also, so that the passage has become as it were part of a liturgy whenever the
destruction of a woodland is involved. Round about 1936 or 1940 I first heard the
Ennius fragment read aloud and the *sound* of the Latin words haunted me and
although I could apprehend the meaning only *very* partially and patchily, I *felt*
that surely form and content were marvellously wed and a subsequent reading of a
translation confirmed my feelings. However, when in 1967 I wished to evoke some
part of this passage it was clearly necessary to again consult a translation, and also
a friend with a knowledge of Latin which I have not. Further I found it necessary
to replace *securibus* by *rapacibus* in that my trees were brought down not 'by axes'
but 'by tusks' and similarly *magnas quercus* would not do because none of the oaks
of the Welsh hill-site I had in mind are by any means 'great' or 'mighty', but, on
the contrary, strangling and stunted, so I replaced *magnas* by *sacras* seeing that in so
far as one is concerned for and stands within the mythus of this island, the oak, of
whatever sort, great or small, has for obvious reasons, sacral associations.
[2] Trwyth: pronounce troóith.

tendoned roots of the trees of the *llwyn* whereby are the tallest with the least levelled low and lie up so down.

It is the great *ysgithrau*[1] of the *porcus Troit* that have stove in the wattled walls of the white dwellings, it is he who has stamped out the seed of fire, shattered the *pentan*[2] stone within the dwellings; strewn the green leaf bright limbs with the broken white limbs of the folk of the dwellings, so that the life sap of the flowers of the forest mingles the dark life sap of the fair bodies of the men who stood in the trackway of the long tusked great hog, *y twrch dirfawr ysgithrog hir*.[3]

Tawny black sky scurries
                              low over
Ysgyryd[4] hill
and over the level topped heights
                              of Mynnydd Pen y fal[5]
                              cold is wind
                              grey is rain, but
                              BRIGHT IS CANDELA
where this lord is in slumber.

Are his wounded ankles
                              lapped with the ferric waters
that all through the night
                              hear the song
from the night dark seams
                              where the narrow skulled *caethion*[6]
labour the changing shifts
                              for the cosmocrats of alien lips
in all the fair lands

[1] *ysgithrau*: tusks. Pronounce approximately us gith rei.

[2] *pentan*: hearth. Pronounce pén tan.

[3] *y twrch dirfawr ysgithrog hir*: the huge hog, long tusked. Pronounce approximately uh toorch deerr vowrr us gith rog heerr.

[4] Ysgyryd: pronounce us gúh rid.

[5] Mynnydd Pen y fal: pronounce mun ith pen uh vál; commonly known as 'The Sugar Loaf'. The Welsh name of this mountain means 'the head of the summit'.

[6] *caethion*: slaves. Pronounce approximately keith ('ei' as in height) ee on.

                    of the dark measures under
(from about Afon Lwyd
                    in the confines of green Siluria
westward to where the naiad of the *fons* head
                    pours out the Lesser Gwendraeth[1]
high in the uplands
                    above Ystrad Tywi[2]
and indeed further
                    west & south of Merlin's Caer
even in the lost cantrevs
                    of spell held Demetia
where was Gorsedd Arberth,[3] where the *palas*[4] was
                    where the prince who hunted
met the Prince of Hunters
                    in his woof of grey
and gleam pale dogs
                    not kennelled on earth floor
lit the dim chase.)

Is the Usk a drain for his gleaming tears
who weeps for the land
                    who dreams his bitter dream
for the folk of the land
does Tawe[5] clog for his sorrows
do the parallel dark seam drainers
                    mingle his anguish stream
with the scored valleys' tilted refuse.
Does his freight of woe
                    flood South by East
on Sirhywi[6] and Ebwy[7]

[1] Gwendraeth: pronounce approximately gwén dreith ('ei' as in height).
[2] Ystrad Tywi: The Vale of Towy. Pronounce approximately ustrad túh wee.
[3] Gorsedd Arberth: pronounce approximately gorr seth ('th' as in breathe) árr berrth, ('er' as in errand).
[4] *palas*: *palace*. Pronounce pál lass.
[5] Tawe: pronounce approximately tau eh.
[6] Sirhywi: pronounce approximately seerr húh ee.
[7] Ebwy: pronounce éb wee.

                              is it southly bourn
on double Rhondda's fall to Taff?[1]

    Do the stripped boughs grapple
above the troubled streams
                         when he dream/fights
his nine/day's fight
                         which he fought alone
with the hog in the Irish wilderness
                         when the eighteen twilights
                         and the ten midnights
and the equal light of the nine mid/mornings
were equally lit
                         with the light of the saviour's fury
and the dark fires of the hog's eye
which encounter availed him nothing.

                         Is his royal anger ferriaged
where black/rimed Rhymni
                         soils her Marcher/banks
                         Do the bells of St. Mellon's
toll his dolour
                         are his sighs canalled
where the mountain/ash
                         droops her bright head
for the black pall of Merthyr?

Do Afan[2] and Nedd[3] west it away
does grimed Ogwr[4] toss on a fouled ripple
his broken/heart flow

                         out to widening Hafren[5]
                         and does she, the Confluence Queen
queenly bear on her spume/frilled frock

[1] Taff: pronounce taf, the 'a' is short.   [2] Afan: pronounce áv/van.
[3] Nedd: pronounce very approximately nathe, as in lathe or bathe.
[4] Ogwr: pronounce og/oorr.   [5] Hafren: (Sabrina) pronounce háv/ren.

a maimed king's sleep bane?
                    Do the long white hands
would you think, of the Brides of the Déssi
                    unloose galloòns
to let the black tress⁄stray
                    web the pluvial Westerlies
does the vestal flame in virid⁄hilled Kildare
                    renew from secret embers
the undying fire
                    that sinks on the Hill Capitoline
    Does the wake⁄dole mingle the cormorant scream
does man⁄*sídhe* to fay⁄queen bemoan
the passage of a king's griefs, westing far
                    out to moon⁄swayed Oceanus
    Does the blind & unchoosing creature of sea know the
marking and indelible balm from flotsomed sewage and the
seaped valley⁄waste?
    Does the tide⁄beasts' maw
                    drain down the princely tears
with the mullocked slag⁄wash
                    of Special Areas?
Can the tumbling and gregarious porpoises
does the aloof and infrequent seal
                    that suns his puckered back
                    and barks from Pirus' rock
tell the dole⁄tally of a drowned *taeog* from a
Gwledig's golden collar, refracted in Giltar shoal?

    Or, is the dying gull
                    on her sea⁄hearse
that drifts the oily bourne
                    to tomb at turn of tide
her own stricken cantor?
Or is it for the royal tokens
                    that with her drift
that the jagg'd and jutting *morben*[1] echoes

---

[1] *morben*: headland. Pronounce morr⁄ben.

and the deep hollows of *yr ogof*[1] echo
and the hollow eddies echo:

        Dirige, dirige[2]

and out, far, far beyond
on thalassic Brendan's heaving trackway
to unknown *insulae*

        where they sing
their west In Paradisums[3]

        and the corposants toss
for the dying flax-flame

        and West-world glory
in transit is.

But yet he sleeps:

        when he shifts a little in his fitfull
slumber does a covering stone dislodge

        and roll to Reynoldstone?
When he fretfully turns

        crying out in a great voice
        in his fierce sleep-anger
does the habergeon'd sentinel

        alert himself sudden
from his middle-watch doze

        in the crenelled traverse-bay
of the outer bailey wall

        of the *castell*[4] these Eingl-Ffrancwyr[5]
call in their lingua La Haie Taillée
that the Saeson[6] other ranks

        call The Hay
(which place is in the tongue of the men of the land,
Y Gelli Gandryll, or, for short, Y Gelli)

[1] *yr ogof*: the cave. Pronounce ur óg-ov.
[2] First Antiphon at Matins for the Dead, *Dirige, Domine, Deus meus, in conspectu tuo viam meam.*
[3] Burial Service, Roman Rite Antiphon. '*In paradisum deducant te Angeli*' etc.
[4] *castell*: castle. Pronounce approximately cáss-tell, 'll' represents the Welsh *ll*.
[5] Eingl-Ffrancwyr: Anglo-Frenchmen. Pronounce approximately ain-gl-fránc-weirr. [6] Saeson: Englishmen. Pronounce approximately seis-on.

Does he cock his weather/ear, enquiringly
lest what's on the west wind
                        from over beyond the rising contours
may signify that in the broken
                tir y blaenau[1]
these broken dregs of Troea
                        yet again muster?
Does he nudge his drowsing mate?
                        Do the pair of them
say to each other: 'Twere not other
than wind/cry, for sure – yet
                        best to warn the serjeant below.
He'll maybe
                        warn the Captain of the Watch
or some such
                        and he, as like as not
may think best to rouse the Castellan
                        – that'll please him
in his newly glazed, arras/hung chamber
                        with his Dean/coal fire
nicely blazing
snug with his dowsabel
                        in the inner keep
Wont improve his temper, neither, come the morrow
with this borough and hereabouts alerted
                        and all for but a wind/bluster.
Still, you never know, so
                        best stand on Standing Orders
and report to them as has the serjeancy
the ordering and mandate, for
you never know, mate:
                        wind/stir may be, most like to be
as we between us do agree
                        or – stir of gramarye
or whatsomever of ferly – who should say?
                        or solid substantiality?

[1] *tir y blaenau*: land of the border uplands. Pronounce approximately teerr uh
blein/ei.

you never know *what* may be
                              – not hereabouts.
No wiseman's son *born* do know
                              not in these whoreson March-lands
of this Welshry.

Yet he sleeps on
                              very deep is his slumber:
how long has he been the sleeping lord?
are the clammy ferns
                              his rustling vallance
does the buried rowan
                              ward him from evil, or
does he ward the tanglewood
                              and the denizens of the wood
are the stunted oaks his gnarled guard
                              or are their knarred limbs
strong with his sap?
Do the small black horses
                              grass on the hunch of his shoulders?
are the hills his couch
                              or is he the couchant hills?
Are the slumbering valleys
                              him in slumber
                              are the still undulations
the still limbs of him sleeping?
Is the configuration of the land
                              the furrowed body of the lord
are the scarred ridges
                              his dented greaves
do the trickling gullies
                              yet drain his hog-wounds?
Does the land wait the sleeping lord
                              or is the wasted land
that very lord who sleeps?

November 1966 to March 1967.

from THE BOOK OF BALAAM'S ASS

The following pages are included here as a fragment of a much longer writing, or rather pieces of writings, made in the late 1930s and early 1940s.

'In Parenthesis': begun in 1928 and nearing completion by about 1934 was delayed by illness from being submitted to the publisher and so did not appear until June 1937. About that time I had begun on further fragments consisting of very diverse content. These I provisionally called 'The Book of Balaam's Ass'. This collection I decided to abandon altogether. But parts of it were a harking back to conversations of the immediately post-1914-18 period and to the later phases of the conflict itself.

The pages included here are taken practically en bloc from one such passage. In part because while written in the 1930s and '40s it evokes conversations of 1919-20 and, as I say above, the later phases of the war itself and immediately subsequent converse, while at the same time is indicative of trends, which some years later and however differently conditioned, have something in common with 'The Anathemata'.

Anyway, for good or ill, these few pages from one section of the abandoned 'Book of Balaam's Ass' were chosen as seeming to afford a link of sorts between the two widely separated books: 'In Parenthesis' and 'The Anathemata'.

. . . regular at the rails, smilers at flag-day corners, blameless, not extortionate, superior to party, not loving their own selves, bird-watchers and inventors of humane bull-slaying, temperate, fair-spoken, appreciative – all this and a great deal more – it arouses complicated emotions to see such intimate friends unawares seated confidently in a ventilated room smiling at superstition on the fifth of November. May be they'll yet laugh on the other side of their faces at gunpowdered reason.

I know it bores you Cicily, and you too, Pamela-born-between-the-sirens, but Bertie will corroborate what I'm saying, and you ask poor Clayton. Willy and Captain Varley never used any other analogies, and Belle Varley takes it like a lamb, and even asks intelligent questions between her dropped stitches

– about all kinds of details about what the 5th did when Theodore Vaughan-Herbert – ('Taffy' for short) caught a nasty one in the abortive raid, east of Hulluch – O yes I was, I was with Taffy for a while, only we differed in glory, but I expect he'd know me. It's all very well to yawn and let the dead bury the 6,000 mental cases still under observation – (that's the figure for October 1937 anyway). Yes I know the next packet will make it all seem silly, like Spud Bullen's unwearied and graphic account of an assegai's accurate trajectory and penetrating down drive, was to us when he told, re-told and developed his tale in a rocking cubby-hole with a box-barrage down. Poor boring old Spud, the tedious old sweat – like Emeritus Nodens of the 2nd Adjutrix who regaled them with tales of the elusive Pict (with half his face vermillion) that burned through the creeping brume sleuthing white for the native night of that Ultimate Province. They came over he said in front of Vercovicium he said.

Further forward, in the signal stations he'd heard tell it was about as mirk-lit as the inside of a Capitol wolf. He supposed the Otadini came cat-eyed from birth – for their woaded limbs open from womb-dark onto a connatural gloom.

Well, no, he couldn't say he had properly speaking, but he'd met a man from the Victrix whose statement could be relied upon and after all it was their sector in the normal run of things. On the other hand a mate of his had a very different tale to tell, asserting that it was as fair a land as could be asked for, and put the question: How could the mirk not be less as each milliaria north brings a man more under the influence of Celestial Arcturus, 'Ursus the Bear of the Island and our constant light' the natives say.

He'd keep up this topic whether you liked it or not – you couldn't choose but hear – sometimes he'd borrow his thrills from Pontus in Asia, then you were cooked. I ask you – what can exceed the tedium of twice-told tales from East of Suez especially when
they come to the phenomena of levitation, of the solitary and invisible spear that bolts from the meridien sky every third day, the one amphora of sherbert for a month of sundays for each half cohort and – O! Cripes – he's commenced on the camels – their hostility to man, their peculiar aversions and perfections,

especially when you
are cornered for a thousand and one nights. I've known him keep
up this topic till closing time, with Clitus so bored and Crixus
so tight, and Marcella poor child, yawning and twisting her
silken maniple – but there was no stopping him.

But it is inevitable and meet:
while there is breath it's only right to bear immemorial wit
ness.
   There were breakings of thin ice I can tell you and incomings
to transmute the whole dun envelope of this flesh.
   We have seen transfigurations on a plain, swiftly and slowing,
unsheafing slow like beggar-shifts king's hands make fall from
secret queens.
   That's what it was like sometimes – a slow discovering –
night by night (the slow days raced)
   But night: at night the veils were drawn slowly for you to
see the limbs there; it was at night they spangled the clods with
stars and lit torches for the humble and meek. It was at night I
saw the weedy, white, ex-clerk, – dead as a nail, for sure, left at
the sap-head and he standing upright between two, armed at all
points and he himself, too, crowned with iron and bearing the
weight of it, smiling in the brazier-flare, coming and falling
gustily with the down-draught play in the windy place.
   You Bertie, Leslie, 'Waladr, Joe, Griffin, Lamkin, Hob,
Malkin, Warwick, Talbot, – you Hector, whose arse they
couldn't see for dust at the circuit of the wall – the bastards got
you in the end. You will be my witness who knew how the
leaden clay could flame, you who saw the hundred thousand
shopkeepers in glistening scape-goat hauberks.
   Tilly-vally Mr Pistol that's a petty tale of y'r Gallia wars.
Gauffer it well and troupe it fine, pad it out to impressive pro-
portions, grace it from the ancients. Gee! I do like a bloody lie
turned gallantly romantical, fantastical, glossed by the old gang
from the foundations of the world. Press every allusion into your
Ambrosian racket, ransack the sacred canon and have by heart
the sweet Tudor magician, gather your sanctions and weave
your allegories, roseate your lenses, serve up the bitter dregs in

silver-gilt, bless it before and behind and swamp it with baptismal and continual dew.

No, Livinia, won't wash, and that you know well enough. To adopt the initial formula, 'Ladies and gentlemen, I will re-move the hat.' You will observe the golden lily-flowers powdered to drape a million and a half disembowelled yeanlings.

There's a sight for you that is in our genuine European tradi-tion.

Lime-wash over the tar-brush?

No, but rather, cistern the waters of Camelot to lave your lousy linen. The salient is Broceliande, these twain indeed are one.

Here we have the windmill. There you see the advancing hero. The structure is of re-inforced concrete, the loop-holes are of the best pattern and well disposed so as to afford the maximum sweep of fire, the approaches are secured by a treble belt and his trip-wire is as cunningly staked as only he knows how. It's stockaded and aproned; he's shovelled his gabions tight for his supports to come secure – trust him to leave no stone unturned. It's as level as Barking and as bare as your palm, as trapped and decoyed as a Bannockburn frontage for 300 yards from below his glacis.

All the fine fiery waters in Headquarter's larder won't raise a mole-hill for Lieutenant Fairy on that open plain, where he's detailed, in the inscrutable counsels, to make a soldier's fall. He can take thought if he likes from now till zero, he won't add a cubit of cover for himself nor all his franks, not for:
his bosom and intimate china
2nd Lieutenant Jack Smart
not a bush, no brick-bat, not any accidental & advantageous fold, no lie of dead ground the length of a body for his trusted prompter and expert in war: Sergeant Varro, nor his second, the paid man of fortune Sgt. Michael Mary Gabriel Olav Aumerle from Sord Colum Cille of the dark tribes of the Féni, long, long since inter-meddled with the blond wolves in with the surf-break from Nord Meer o'er the faem via mareel'd Zetland & the Orcades, by Out Isles of Abendsee and making south by east through the North Channel for Sud Isles & Mannaw.

Larboard now, to leeward[1]
the blackguard Hill of Howth making Eblana Bay to the Hurdle
Town.
Of such stock was Colour-Sergeant Aumerle, D.C.M., M.M.

Not a rock to cleft for, not a spare drift of soil for the living
pounds of all their poor bodies drowned in the dun sea.
For:
Corporal Oliver of No. 1 nor for
Corporal Amis and
Lance Corporal Amile of No. 2, nor for signaller Balin and his
incompatible mess-mate linesman Balan (there was a marriage
compounded of impediments, dirempt and other from each
where these two buddies from the word go – they tore No. 3 in
a faction again and often.)
Nor for Lance Corporal Holt, nor his sly, insubordinate, most
secret butty – Pte. Heath, nor for Lance Corporal Bawdock the
laughing leader of No. 4, nor for
'66 Adam and
'66 Bell
nor for '22 Hilton and '55 Rolle who marched without talking,
who 'listed from countrysides unknown to each other, but of
whom Nosey Tupper said: Two jokers from one womb, I warrant.
Nor for Clym of the Clough and Gisbourne and Goodfellow
who plucked and roasted the Picardy gander on the evening of
the show, behind Neuf Berquin; the appurtenances they con-
sumed with fire, the fire they kindled with seasoned wood, the
wood they lifted entire was Ma'm'selle Milkduck's byre door.
(And Christ – her rage when she ran for the Redcap.) They left
no trace but a cinder ring for the dew to avoid – but there's no
cover for them either, nor for their grease-lined bellies.
Nor for '14 Bullcalf that Armourer-Sergeant Brackenbury
clinked for asking for two dinners on one plate – poor little
Calfy, he took the gloss literally, but he knew the official defini-
tion in front of the Mill, because of Ober-Leutnant Bebba's
parabellum.

[1] Pronounce 'larboard' lar-b'rd. Pronounce 'leeward' lew'rd.

Nor for

Goater

Grover

Bunker and

Cobb

the Jutish heavies, who murmured into their bivouac sheets of narrow tillage and divided inheritance – Oh, yes, b'gavelkind they hold – the same as the Wealas.

Nor yet for

Loddington

Weeden or

Grimsdall

who mouthed inarticulate words at the latter end of the binge at Fleubaix, of Hycga[1] their tall father, who burned twelve Welsh-men with fire in Piggots garth and had his oats in Speen.

These three chair-makers' mates moved lightfoot from Fricourt to Highwood saying: There's nothing like chalk to dance on. But there was no help for them either.

Machinengwehrschütze Balder Helige, with his little gun, got them all three with the tail of his traverse.

Nor for Willy Hall, who left his lambs up spout and got 'pressed in parlour at Burnsall together with masher Willy Cawdor.

Nor for '16 Nicholay whose branded arse made him a jape at M.O.'s inspection, nor for his towny '02 Absolon, who laughed up his cardigan sleeve, who kept for his joy the Sergeant Carpenter's gentle bird, the Popinjay of La Clytte, three days and three nights in the hay-loft above Snob Springer's shop and fed her on citron and bully, and white wine and bread.

A few others were in on this scandal and Lieutenant Lovelace and 2nd Lieutenant, the Honourable Lucian Piert Walters looked suspiciously awkward for their elevated and disinterested status; and when it all came out C.Q.M.S. Snook gave his

[1] In the 1940s, when writing this passage I supposed my source could only be the *A.S. Chronicle*. But on enquiries I'm told that no such entry exists in the *Chronicle*. Jutes in the vicinity of High-Wycombe sounds improbable, but on the other hand, the idea was fixed in my mind and one does not invent tales of this sort, *ex nibilo*.

evidence with a wry look – but the tumult of war stilled their uncharity.

Wig Muckermann's minnie emptied flame and mingled steel, like the grievous hail, like the wounding towers that dilapidate impartial death alike on cuckold and goat. So it was with the Popinjay's clients – they all went up together in one burst before the mill; and the other names inscribed on that particular packet were:

three poor men
bible punchers
whose souls are with Jesus:
Tom Bradshaw
Skinny Bowditch
Ebenezer Wrench, who stepped from his gospeller's tub in Tiggy's Fields to join the East Surreys, but was subsequently transferred, and with them: Harry Gill, who wore under his service jacket, his issue cardigan and another he'd stolen, and two waistcoats above his issue shirt; and under it a woven vest of lamb's wool and next to his goosey skin a body-belt twice-tied (Chittie Tuckbacon swore he'd seen the poor sin-bearer shiver over his steaming skilly in a mid-August trench and Isaac Prosser whispered: Iesu Mawr![1] It takes a powerful spell, man, to work such unnatural ill on a person's body. And Punic Trelawny, his Cornwealas confidant, said the platoon would come to no good, but shipwreck, with so cursed a hand on board; and God damn such a shaker said Major Thwaites. B'Jasus, there's bane some oppression for sartain said Captain Geraldine Purcell.)

He was parted from Bradshaw, Bowditch, and Wrench in middle-air by the separating arm of a woman, carrying faggots, who leaned from the moon.[2]

Nor yet was there aid or covering wing, or upright, or linden hedge or agger or paraduct or mothering skirt for a frighted last-born, or gunnal for the evil swell; or anything drawn to mask or shadow, or brunt-bearing mound of salvation, nor any sweet flowing water to check the scent, or any device to stay a ravening

---

[1] Iesu Mawr, 'Great Jesus', pronounce Iesu as approximately yess-ee, accent on first syllable.
[2] Cf. Wordsworth's 'Goody Blake and Harry Gill'.

pursuer, or conduit or sewer for a felon's joy, or blanket for head for dark imagining in an evil tower, nor your scutum for his trauma, nor any go-between nor ballast to jettison to rectify the deadly list on her, nor cool and immediate dock for nettle in that hedgeless field, nor any reef to take the outer squall. And what of His sure mercies that He swore in the ancient days – where is His tempering for our bare back and sides – where is provided the escape on that open plain?

You'd like a pavise to tortoise you to move with your mates like a wall against his liquid pitch, or the locked shields that determined the boundaries of western man – or an hare's form for your kicking hind legs would be something. The foxes have holes but

Tommy Tucker

'O2 Snug

John Plowman

have Sweet Fanny Adams when Hieronymous Högemann feeds his Big Willie[1] in Aachen Alley and Rembalt the Galician pulls the string. There will be no failing of fuses or charges on their part.

Iselin, too, with his adjustable sights for his cumbrous weapon grinned through his concrete slit to see:

Dai Meyrick and Madoc Sey searching for a mountain. (For it was the property of these men that they would not walk on the level except by compulsion.)

But there was no help for them on that open plain.

Iselin it was also who accounted for Langland and Rhymer and Byrde, because they looked this way and that for a green lane. (For it was the property of these men that they would always walk where grass was.) There was no help for them either on that open plain because the virtue of the land was perished and there was not grass but only broken earth and low foliage of iron; and from the tangled spread of the iron hedge hung the garments peculiar to the men of Ireland and their accoutrements, and the limbs and carcases of the Irish were stretched on some of the iron bushes,

[1] 'Big Willie', the heaviest type of German trench-mortars were sometimes called by us 'Big Willies' after the name of Kaiser Wilhelm II, and those of lighter calibre, 'Little Willies' after the Crown-prince.

because the men of Ireland had made an attempt on the Mill in the early Spring of '15 and again in high summer by express command of the G.O.C. in C. So that the Mill was named on English trench maps: Irish Mill, but on enemy maps it was called Aachen Haus. And as there was no help for the men of Ireland so there was no help for the men of Britain.

Further forward and under his very nose were also bleached rags hanging, and with field-glasses it was possible to discern in those cobwebs the chequered cloth of the men of Lower Britain, because earlier still the men of Lower Britain had occupied for some hours a drain, called after them: Jock's Folly. But there had been no help for them either because the configuration of the land was such that it had been the simplest thing in the world for the men in Aachen Haus to dislodge them, and make their ditch quite flat with heavy mortars operating from Aachen Alley and Aachen Support. It was by express command of the G.O.C. in C., that the men of Lower Britain had been sent forward to hold their drain in the early summer of '15 and of whom only three returned, and by the same command the men of Ireland had made their attempt in the Autumn of the same year as in the previous Spring and it was by the same command that Mr Fairy and his men from Upper Britain made their diversion. And three men only returned from this diversion, and they were called:
Private Lucifer
Private Shenkin
Private Austin
and the reason for their invulnerability was this: Pte. Lucifer (Squib Lucifer he was called in his section) was possessed of agility, subtlety and lightness, so that however often Hans Iselin screwed up his left eye and however precise his aim and however accurate his special sights, and with whatever dispatch he co-ordinated his movements, Pte. Lucifer stood upright under his fire the most beautifullest of men laughing like anything, so that there seemed to be added to the properties before mentioned that other, against which not sharp steel nor swift lead nor any chemical discharge is of any avail. It seemed to Hans Iselin and to Balder Helige and to Ober-Leutnant Bebba, and indeed to Hauptmann Otto von Altdorfer that Pte. Lucifer was possessed of the quality

of impassibility. So that afterwards, in their reserve implacements, Bebba would confide alone to Hauptmann Altdorfer: 'How, sir, should we contend against *Geister*? That Tommy, sir, was no infantryman, but an Annointed Cherub.' Maybe, Leutnant, may be, the enemy recruit widely.

And that is the reason why he was called one of the three who escaped in the diversion before the Mill. And as before he was called Squib Lucifer, so afterwards he was called Pussy Lucifer, because he escaped the ninth death.

And the reason for the invulnerability of Pte. Shenkin (Pick-em-up Shenkin he was called by his section) is that he was the least sure-footed of men, and the most ungainly and the most easily confused of any man of the Island of Britain, and the most slow to make his extremities do what his stomach or brain desired, and the most forgetful of men, and when he slept no one knew at what hour he would awaken; nevertheless he was possessed of a certain guile and there was in his maladroitness an innate scheme of self-preservation, and his stumbling often saved him from reaching a disastrous goal. And when he stumbled in the morning it was never certain if he would regain his feet before sunset (for after sunset, he said, a man can walk with more composure) or if he mislaid his jack-knife or his hold-all or his camp-comforter it was not certain for how long the parade might be left standing, or the Orderly Sergeants blowing and stamping before he would recover them – for it was his ingrained habit not to move without these articles of kit, unless he were compelled by violence or by the express command of Sergeant Varro.

Now it so happened that he stumbled half-way-over into a shallow crater where his intricate equipment easily entangled itself so as to mesh his floundering limbs in a discarded concertina of wire. Now partly because he had no effective interest in the G.O.C. in C.'s diversion before the Mill, and partly because of his inability to deal with any complicated derangement of things, and partly because of his very great and continual fear, he re-mained as quiet as a rodent in his burrow of salvation, and over his drawn-back ears and unseen to his deflected eyes the missiles wove this way and that a steel thatch for him. And once the studded heel of Squib Lucifer darkened his snuggery, and he heard, above the noise of the weapons, familiar laughter on the plain.

When it was quite dark and there was no sound at all except of a difficult breathing coming up from the earth, and inter-mittently the half-cries of those who would call strongly from their several and lonely places, on
that Creature of Water, or on
some creature of their own kind by name, as on
gentle Margaret on
Amy, on Gwenfrewi
on Bella on Donnabelle
on Aunt Birch on
Ned
long dead, on dead old Elfed, on great-uncle George, on Brigit the Kildare maid that kindled the fires for Billy of Clonmor in the *hortus* of Iverna. On Joan the maid that keeled the pots beyond the baize doors at Mrs Jack Horners. Or on those Bright ones to whose particular cults they were dedicate.
On God the Father of Heaven because with Him there is neither wounding nor unwounding. On God the Word because by Him we know the wound and the salve, on God the Life Giver because His workings are never according to plan and because of the balm under his Wing, and because by Him even the G.O.C. in C.'s diversion before the Mill can shine with the splendour of order. The Sanctifier and bright Lord who is glorious in operation, the dispositioner, the effector of all trans-substantiations, who sets the traverse wall according to the measure of the angel with the reed, who knows best how to gather his epiklesis from that open plain, who transmutes their cheerless blasphemy into a lover's word, who spoke by Balaam and by Balaam's ass, who spoke also by Sgt. Bullcock.

On the Lamb because He was slain.

On the Word seen by men because He was familiar with the wounding iron.

On the Son of Man because He could not carry the cross-beam of his *stauros*.

On the Son of Mary, because, like Perédur, He left His Mother to go for a soldier, for he would be a *miles* too.

On Mary because of her secret piercing, and because, but for her pliant *Fiat mihi*, no womb-burden to joust with the fiend in the lists of Hierosolyma, in his fragile habergeon: HUMANA NATURA.[1]

On the Angel in skins because the soldiers asked him a question.

On the key-man, the sword-bearer, because he lied to a nosey girl and warmed his hands at a corporal's brazier.

On the chosen three because they slept at their posts.

On the God of the philosophers who is not in the fire, but who yet can make fire.

On Enoch's shining companion who walks by your side like an intimate confederate, who chooses suddenly, so that the bearers look in vain for your body, who takes you alive to be his perpetual friend.

On Abraham's God who conditions his vows, who elects his own, who plucks out by tribe and sub-tribe and gens and family. On the Dux Pacis

Unben Ariel Fryn

Urddol[2] arbennig of Uru-height[3]

sine genealogia, with neither beginning of time

nor end of days, assimilatus autem Filio Dei

MELCHISÉDEC[4] Wledig, he who

two millennia before the Abendmahl

foretokened that Oblation made on dies Iovis

noswyl duw Gwener[5]

[1] Cf. Langland's *Piers Plowman* 'B' Text, Passus xviii, lines 22–23.

[2] The Welsh *U* is pronounced approximately 'ee' as in 'peer'. So Unben (a ruler or leader) is pronounced een-ben, and Urddol (a consecrated priest) is pronounced eer-thol, 'th' as in 'then'. Arbennig means principle or chief, so Urddol arbennig equates with *summus sacerdos*, the title of Melchisedec in the Canon of the Mass.

[3] The 'U' in Uru-height is as that in Zulu.

[4] The stress accent on 'e' in Melchisedec is merely in accord with the stress on the penultimate syllable in the majority of Welsh words and because it seemed to go with the Welsh title Gwledig (a ruler of great eminence). Cf. Cunedda Wledig, Macsen Wledig. Taliesin refers to God as *Gwledig Nef a phob tud*, 'Ruler of Heaven and all countries'.

[5] noswyl duw Gwener = *In Vigilia dies Veneris,* that is *dies Iovis*, in Welsh dydd (or duw) Ionawr. The Thursday of the *In supremæ nocte cœnæ* of Aquinas' superb hymn.

the day he was to suffer

pridie the Ides of Mars[1]

about the time when bough begins to frond

and stella'd aconite brights holt-edge

where men axe down the Dreaming lignum

against to-morrow's Immolation

in the first month

of the Romulean year Ab Urbe Condita

seven hundred and eighty-four.

By Levitic intercalation

the Eve of the Preparation Day of

the Feast of Transit

a Dies Magna of obligation

for the gens Iudaica.

Feria V (in Cena Domini) of the Great Week.

Twenty centuries of waste land back

this summus sacerdos and Rex Salem

had foreshewn, under the same signa

of Ceres fractured, of

Liber made confluent with

this, thy creature of water

yn y Caregl Rhagorol.[2]

[1] In the old Roman calendar March was the first month, as it was also among the Celtic peoples and in the Livitical code. In that month the Ides fell on the 15th day so I felt justified in referring to the day of the Crucifixion as 'pridie the Ides of Mars'. But I wish to make it clear that this, along with *noswyl duw Gwener*, for the Thursday feast on 'the day before he suffered', are in no sense meant to have any historicity. The year of the Paschal period in which the Passion occurred is un-known. There is great uncertainty and confusion as to when the meal of unleavened bread, the 'azymes', stood in relation to the actual Passover which according to Jewish law had to be on the 14th day of Nisan, but for various causes intercalation had to be made whereby the Feast of the Passover could be as late as some date in what we call April. I have simply followed the tradition of the Church and sup-posed the Supper at which the Oblation placed the Offerand in the state of a Victim to be immolated on the morrow, i.e. Dies Veneris, which *if* it was in the Roman month of March would be the day before the Ides and by Jewish reckoning on the eve of the Passover. But there are further complexities which cannot be gone into here. Similarly in giving the year as A.U.C. 784, that is one of the various years thought by some to be the year of the Passion, but that too presents difficul-ties and I used it here before I was aware of the extreme complexities involved.

[2] yn y Caregl rhagorol. yn (in) pronounced 'un' as in 'under', y (definite

On all the devices of the peoples, on all anointed stones, on fertile goddesses, that covering arbours might spring up on that open plain for poor maimed men to make their couches there.

On her that wept for a wounded palm that she got by a mortal spear – that she might salve a gaping groin that the race might not be without generation.

On the unknown God.

Each calling according to what breasts had fed them – for rite follows matriarchate[1] when y'r brain-pan's stove in.

That's why he heard Dai Meyrick make his dolorous ana-phora, like the cry of a wounded hare, on Magons and Maponus, because his mother was of the line of Caw of North Britain and her love was beyond the Wall with the Men of the North (albeit she sat under her husband in his Moravian bethel, at Drws-y-Coed-Uchaf in Arfon in the apostasy of the latter days).

Pick-em-up Shenkin could stand this no longer. He found that his wire mesh slipped away from him easily. In his covert he had not been altogether ungraced because of the diverse cries coming up from the earth, and because of the baptism by coward-ice which is more terrible than that of water or blood. Remember-ing the Rocky Mountain goat he leapt from shell-hole to shell-hole (and no one could tell whether he leapt because he feared or feared because he leapt) until he regained the security of the assembly trench. And that is why he is called one of the three who escaped from the diversion before the Mill.

The invulnerability of Pte. Austin was by reason of the suff-rages of his mother who served God hidden in a suburb, and because of her the sons of the women in that suburb were believed to be spared bodily death at that time, because she was believed to be appointed mediatrix there. And it was urged by some that

article) pronounced approximately as in the expletive 'uh', Caregl (chalice) pro-nounced 'car-regl' – 'gl' as in English 'angle', rhagorol (excelling in splendour) pronounced 'rha-gorol' (accent on middle syllable). I use this Welsh form because it chances that, in the Latin *præclarus Calix* or *præclarum Calicem* in the Canon of the Mass, the word 'præclarum', being found by the translators of the new verna-cular English Mass to have no equivalent in idiomatic English, was either left out or 'excellent' made to serve. The Welsh form *rhagoral* is not only idiomatic but gives the sense of *præclarus* and evokes some of the splendour required.

[1] Cf. the principle of the Xtian Ecclesia: Rite follows Patriarchate.

Mrs Austin conditioned and made acceptable in some round⟋
about way the tomfoolery of the G.O.C. in C. Anyway it was
by reason of her suffrages that Private Austin was called one of
the three who escaped from the diversion before the Mill.

And as before he was named by his section Ducky Austin,
so afterwards he was called Austin the Dodger.

But for all the rest there was no help on that open plain.